Basilikon doron, or, King James's instructions to his dearest sonne, Henry the Prince, now reprinted, by His Majesties command (1682)

King of England James I

Basilikon doron, or, King James's instructions to his dearest sonne, Henry the Prince, now reprinted, by His Majesties command

Basilikon doron
James I, King of England, 1566-1625.
Marginal notes.
First edition, 1599.
[31], 102 p. :
London : Printed by M. Flesher for Samuel Mearne ..., 1682.
Wing / J128A
English
Reproduction of the original in the Henry E. Huntington Library and Art Gallery

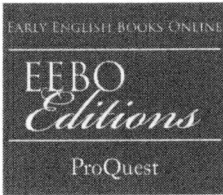

Early English Books Online (EEBO) Editions

Imagine holding history in your hands.

Now you can. Digitally preserved and previously accessible only through libraries as Early English Books Online, this rare material is now available in single print editions. Thousands of books written between 1475 and 1700 and ranging from religion to astronomy, medicine to music, can be delivered to your doorstep in individual volumes of high-quality historical reproductions.

We have been compiling these historic treasures for more than 70 years. Long before such a thing as "digital" even existed, ProQuest founder Eugene Power began the noble task of preserving the British Museum's collection on microfilm. He then sought out other rare and endangered titles, providing unparalleled access to these works and collaborating with the world's top academic institutions to make them widely available for the first time. This project furthers that original vision.

These texts have now made the full journey -- from their original printing-press versions available only in rare-book rooms to online library access to new single volumes made possible by the partnership between artifact preservation and modern printing technology. A portion of the proceeds from every book sold supports the libraries and institutions that made this collection possible, and that still work to preserve these invaluable treasures passed down through time.

This is history, traveling through time since the dawn of printing to your own personal library.

Initial Proquest EEBO Print Editions collections include:

Early Literature

This comprehensive collection begins with the famous Elizabethan Era that saw such literary giants as Chaucer, Shakespeare and Marlowe, as well as the introduction of the sonnet. Traveling through Jacobean and Restoration literature, the highlight of this series is the Pollard and Redgrave 1475-1640 selection of the rarest works from the English Renaissance.

Early Documents of World History

This collection combines early English perspectives on world history with documentation of Parliament records, royal decrees and military documents that reveal the delicate balance of Church and State in early English government. For social historians, almanacs and calendars offer insight into daily life of common citizens. This exhaustively complete series presents a thorough picture of history through the English Civil War.

Historical Almanacs

Historically, almanacs served a variety of purposes from the more practical, such as planting and harvesting crops and plotting nautical routes, to predicting the future through the movements of the stars. This collection provides a wide range of consecutive years of "almanacks" and calendars that depict a vast array of everyday life as it was several hundred years ago.

Early History of Astronomy & Space

Humankind has studied the skies for centuries, seeking to find our place in the universe. Some of the most important discoveries in the field of astronomy were made in these texts recorded by ancient stargazers, but almost as impactful were the perspectives of those who considered their discoveries to be heresy. Any independent astronomer will find this an invaluable collection of titles arguing the truth of the cosmic system.

Early History of Industry & Science

Acting as a kind of historical Wall Street, this collection of industry manuals and records explores the thriving industries of construction; textile, especially wool and linen; salt; livestock; and many more.

Early English Wit, Poetry & Satire

The power of literary device was never more in its prime than during this period of history, where a wide array of political and religious satire mocked the status quo and poetry called humankind to transcend the rigors of daily life through love, God or principle. This series comments on historical patterns of the human condition that are still visible today.

Early English Drama & Theatre

This collection needs no introduction, combining the works of some of the greatest canonical writers of all time, including many plays composed for royalty such as Queen Elizabeth I and King Edward VI. In addition, this series includes history and criticism of drama, as well as examinations of technique.

Early History of Travel & Geography

Offering a fascinating view into the perception of the world during the sixteenth and seventeenth centuries, this collection includes accounts of Columbus's discovery of the Americas and encompasses most of the Age of Discovery, during which Europeans and their descendants intensively explored and mapped the world. This series is a wealth of information from some the most groundbreaking explorers.

Early Fables & Fairy Tales

This series includes many translations, some illustrated, of some of the most well-known mythologies of today, including Aesop's Fables and English fairy tales, as well as many Greek, Latin and even Oriental parables and criticism and interpretation on the subject.

Early Documents of Language & Linguistics

The evolution of English and foreign languages is documented in these original texts studying and recording early philology from the study of a variety of languages including Greek, Latin and Chinese, as well as multilingual volumes, to current slang and obscure words. Translations from Latin, Hebrew and Aramaic, grammar treatises and even dictionaries and guides to translation make this collection rich in cultures from around the world.

Early History of the Law

With extensive collections of land tenure and business law "forms" in Great Britain, this is a comprehensive resource for all kinds of early English legal precedents from feudal to constitutional law, Jewish and Jesuit law, laws about public finance to food supply and forestry, and even "immoral conditions." An abundance of law dictionaries, philosophy and history and criticism completes this series.

Early History of Kings, Queens and Royalty

This collection includes debates on the divine right of kings, royal statutes and proclamations, and political ballads and songs as related to a number of English kings and queens, with notable concentrations on foreign rulers King Louis IX and King Louis XIV of France, and King Philip II of Spain. Writings on ancient rulers and royal tradition focus on Scottish and Roman kings, Cleopatra and the Biblical kings Nebuchadnezzar and Solomon.

Early History of Love, Marriage & Sex

Human relationships intrigued and baffled thinkers and writers well before the postmodern age of psychology and self-help. Now readers can access the insights and intricacies of Anglo-Saxon interactions in sex and love, marriage and politics, and the truth that lies somewhere in between action and thought.

Early History of Medicine, Health & Disease

This series includes fascinating studies on the human brain from as early as the 16th century, as well as early studies on the physiological effects of tobacco use. Anatomy texts, medical treatises and wound treatment are also discussed, revealing the exponential development of medical theory and practice over more than two hundred years.

Early History of Logic, Science and Math

The "hard sciences" developed exponentially during the 16th and 17th centuries, both relying upon centuries of tradition and adding to the foundation of modern application, as is evidenced by this extensive collection. This is a rich collection of practical mathematics as applied to business, carpentry and geography as well as explorations of mathematical instruments and arithmetic; logic and logicians such as Aristotle and Socrates; and a number of scientific disciplines from natural history to physics.

Early History of Military, War and Weaponry

Any professional or amateur student of war will thrill at the untold riches in this collection of war theory and practice in the early Western World. The Age of Discovery and Enlightenment was also a time of great political and religious unrest, revealed in accounts of conflicts such as the Wars of the Roses.

Early History of Food

This collection combines the commercial aspects of food handling, preservation and supply to the more specific aspects of canning and preserving, meat carving, brewing beer and even candy-making with fruits and flowers, with a large resource of cookery and recipe books. Not to be forgotten is a "the great eater of Kent," a study in food habits.

Early History of Religion

From the beginning of recorded history we have looked to the heavens for inspiration and guidance. In these early religious documents, sermons, and pamphlets, we see the spiritual impact on the lives of both royalty and the commoner. We also get insights into a clergy that was growing ever more powerful as a political force. This is one of the world's largest collections of religious works of this type, revealing much about our interpretation of the modern church and spirituality.

Early Social Customs

Social customs, human interaction and leisure are the driving force of any culture. These unique and quirky works give us a glimpse of interesting aspects of day-to-day life as it existed in an earlier time. With books on games, sports, traditions, festivals, and hobbies it is one of the most fascinating collections in the series.

bibliolife
old books. new life.

The BiblioLife Network

This project was made possible in part by the BiblioLife Network (BLN), a project aimed at addressing some of the huge challenges facing book preservationists around the world. The BLN includes libraries, library networks, archives, subject matter experts, online communities and library service providers. We believe every book ever published should be available as a high-quality print reproduction; printed on-demand anywhere in the world. This insures the ongoing accessibility of the content and helps generate sustainable revenue for the libraries and organizations that work to preserve these important materials.

The following book is in the "public domain" and represents an authentic reproduction of the text as printed by the original publisher. While we have attempted to accurately maintain the integrity of the original work, there are sometimes problems with the original work or the micro-film from which the books were digitized. This can result in minor errors in reproduction. Possible imperfections include missing and blurred pages, poor pictures, markings and other reproduction issues beyond our control. Because this work is culturally important, we have made it available as part of our commitment to protecting, preserving, and promoting the world's literature.

GUIDE TO FOLD-OUTS MAPS and OVERSIZED IMAGES

The book you are reading was digitized from microfilm captured over the past thirty to forty years. Years after the creation of the original microfilm, the book was converted to digital files and made available in an online database.

In an online database, page images do not need to conform to the size restrictions found in a printed book. When converting these images back into a printed bound book, the page sizes are standardized in ways that maintain the detail of the original. For large images, such as fold-out maps, the original page image is split into two or more pages

Guidelines used to determine how to split the page image follows:

• Some images are split vertically; large images require vertical and horizontal splits.
• For horizontal splits, the content is split left to right.
• For vertical splits, the content is split from top to bottom.
• For both vertical and horizontal splits, the image is processed from top left to bottom right.

JACOBUS D. G.
Magnæ Brittaniæ
Rex.

R. White sculp.

Sam. Mearne Excudit.

ΒΑΣΙΛΙΚΟΝ ΔΩΡΟΝ.

OR,

King James's

INSTRUCTIONS

To His

DEAREST SONNE,

HENRY

THE

PRINCE.

Now reprinted by His Majesties Command,

LONDON,

Printed by *M. Flesher,* for *Samuel Mearne,* Book-
seller to His Most Excellent MAJESTY,
MDCLXXXII.

THE ARGUMENT.

SONNET.

GOd gives not Kings the ſtile of Gods in vaine,
   For on his Throne his Scepter doe they ſwey:
And as their Subjeƈts ought them to obey,
So Kings ſhould feare and ſerve their God againe.
If then ye would enjoy a happie raigne,
Obſerve the ſtatutes of your heavenly King,
And from his Law, make all your Lawes to ſpring:
Since his Lieutenant here ye ſhould remaine,
Reward the juſt, be ſtedfaſt, true, and plaine,
Repreſſe the proud, maintaining aye the right,
Walke alwaies ſo as ever in his ſight,
Who guards the godly, plaguing the prophane:
   And ſo ye ſhall in Princely vertues ſhine,
   Reſembling right your mightie King Divine.

HENRICUS
Princeps Walliæ etc.

R. White scul.

Sam. Mearne Excudit.

TO
HENRY
My Dearest
SONNE,
And Naturall
SUCCESSOUR.

Whome-to can so rightlie appertaine this booke of instructions to a Prince in all the points of his calling, as well generall, as a Christian towards God; as particular, as a King towards his people? Whome-to, I say, can it so justly appertaine, as unto you my dearest Sonne? Since I the Au-

(a) 4   thour

thour thereof as your naturall
Father, muft be carefull for your
godlie and vertuous education,
as my eldeft Sonne, and the firft
fruits of Gods bleffing towards
me in my pofteritie : and as a
King muft timouflie provide for
your training up in all the points
of a Kings office; fince yee are
my naturall and lawfull fuccef-
for therein : that being rightlie
informed hereby, of the weight
of your burthen, yee may in
time begin to confider, that being borne to be a King, ye are rather borne to *onus,* then *honos:* not
excelling all your people fo farre
in ranke and honour, as in daily
care and hazardous paines-taking,
for the dutifull adminiftration of
that great office, that God hath
laid upon your fhoulders. Laying fo a juft fymmetrie and proportion, betwixt the height of
your honourable place, and the
heavie

heavie weight of your great charge: and confequentlie, in cafe of failing, which God forbid, of the fadneffe of your fall, according to the proportion of that height. I have therefore for the greater eafe to your memorie, and that ye may at the firft, caft up any part that ye have to do with, devided this Treatife in three parts. The firft teacheth you your dutie towards God as a Chriftian: the next, your dutie in your office as a King: and the third informeth you how to behave your felfe in indifferent things, which of themfelves are neither right nor wrong, but according as they are rightlie or wrong ufed; and yet will ferve according to your behaviour therein, to augment or impaire your fame and authoritie at the hands of your people. Receive and welcome this booke then, as
a faith-

a faithfull Preceptour and counfellor unto you: which, becaufe
my affaires will not permit me
ever to be prefent with you, I
ordaine to be a refident faithfull
admonifher of you. And becaufe the howre of death is uncertaine to me, as unto all flefh,
I leave it as my Teftament and
latter-will unto you. Charging
you in the prefence of GOD,
and by the fatherlie authoritie I
have over you, that yee keepe it
ever with you, as carefullie, as
Alexander did the *Iliads* of *Homer.*
Ye will finde it a juft and impar-
tial counfellor; neither flattering
you in anie vice, nor importu-
ning you at unmeete times. It
will not come uncalled, neither
fpeake unfpeered at: and yet
conferring with it when yee are
at quiet, yee fhall fay with *Scipio,*
that yee are *nunquam minùs folus,*
quàm cum folus. To conclude
then,

then, I charge you as ever ye thinke to deſerve my fatherlie bleſſing, to followe and put in practiſe, as farre as lieth in you, the precepts hereafter following. And if yee followe the contrarie courſe, I take the great God to record, that this booke ſhall one day be a witneſſe betwixt me and you; and ſhall procure to be ratified in heaven, the curſe that in that caſe here I give unto you. For I proteſt before that great God, I had rather not bee a Father, and childleſſe, then be a Father of wicked children. But hoping, yea even promiſing unto my ſelfe, that God, who in his great bleſſing ſent you unto me; ſhall in the ſame bleſſing, as he hath given me a Sonne; ſo make him a good and a godlie Sonne; not repenting him of his mercie ſhewed unto me: I end, with

my

my earnest prayer to God, to
worke effectuallie in you, the
fruites of that blessing, which
here from my hart I bestow upon you,

Your loving Father,

J. R.

––––––––––––––––––––––––––

T O

––––––––––––––––––––––––––

eldest Sonne; which I wrote for exercise of my owne ingene, and instruction of him, who is appointed by God (I hope) to sit on my Throne after me. For the purpose and matter thereof being only fit for a King, as teaching him his office; and the person whom-for it was ordayned, a Kings heire, whose secret counsellor and faithfull admonisher it must bee; I thought it no waies convenient, nor comelie, that either it should to all be proclaymed, which to one onely appertained (and specially being a messenger betwixt two so conjunct persons) or yet that the moulde, whereupon he should frame his future behaviour, when he comes both unto the perfection of his yeeres, and possession of his inheritance, should before the hand, bee made common to the people, the subject of his future happie government. And therefore for the more secret, and close keeping of them, I onely permitted seaven of them to be printed, the Printer being first sworn for secrecie: and these seaven I dispersed amongst some of my trustiest servants, to be keeped closelie by them: least in case by the iniquitie, or wearing of time, any of them might have been lost, yet some of them might have remained after me, as witnesses to my Sonne, both of the honest integritie of my heart, and of my fatherlie affection and naturall care towards him.

But

But since contrarie to my intention and expectation, as I have alreadie said, this booke is now vented, and set forth to the publike view of the world, and consequently, subject to every mans censure, as the current of his affection leades him; I am now forced, as well for resisting to the malice of the children of envie, who like Waspes, suckes venome out of every wholsome hearbe; as for the satisfaction of the godly honest sort, in any thing that they may mistake therein; both to publish and spred the true copies thereof, for defacing of the false copies that are alreadie spred, as I am informed: as likewaies, by this Preface, to cleere such parts thereof, as in respect of the concised shortnes of my stile, may be misinterpreted therein.

To come then particularlie to the matter of my booke, there are two speciall great points, which (as I am informed) the malitious sort of men have detracted therein; and some of the honest sort have seemed a little to mistake: whereof the first and greatest is, that some sentences therein should seeme to furnish groundes to men, to doubt of my sinceritie in that Religion, which I have ever constantly professed: the other is, that in some partes thereof, I should seeme to nourish in my minde, a vindictive resolution against England, or at the least, some principalles there, for the Queene my mothers quarrell. *The*

To the Reader.

The firſt calumnie (moſt grievous indeede) is grounded upon the ſharpe and bitter words, that therein are uſed in the deſcription of the humours of Puritanes, and raſhe-headie preachers, that thinke it their honour to contend with Kings, and perturbe whole Kingdomes. The other point is onely grounded upon the ſtraite charge I give my Sonne, not to heare, nor ſuffer any unreverent ſpeeches or bookes againſt any of his parents or progenitors: wherein I doe alleage my owne experience anent the Queene my mother: affirming that I never founde any, that were of perfite age the time of her raigne here; ſo ſtedfaſtly true to me in al my troubles, as theſe that conſtantly kept their allegeance to her in her time. But if the charitable reader will adviſedlie conſider, both the methode and matter of my treatiſe, hee will eaſilie judge, what wrong I have ſuſtained by the carping at both. For my booke, ſuppoſe very ſmall, being devyded in three ſeverall parts; the firſt part thereof onely treates of a Kings duetie towards God in Religion: wherein I have ſo clearlie made profeſſion of my Religion, calling it the Religion wherein I was brought up, and ever made profeſſion of, and wiſhing him ever to continue in the ſame, as the onely true forme of Gods worſhip; that I would have thought my ſincere plainneſſe in that

(b)   firſt

first part upon that subject, should have ditted the mouth of the most envious Momus, *that ever hell did hatche, from barking at any other part of my booke upon that grounde; except they would alledge me to be contrarie to my selfe, which in so small a volume, would smell of too great weaknesse, and sliprinesse of memorie. And the second part of my booke, teaches my sonne howe to use his office, in the administration of justice, and politike government: the third onely contayning a Kings outward behaviour in indifferent things; what aggreeance and conformitie he ought to keepe betwixt his outward behaviour in these things, and the vertuous qualities of his minde: and how they should serve for trunshe-men, to interprete the inwarde disposition of the minde, to the eyes of them that cannot see farther within him, and therefore must onely judge of him by the outward appearance. So as if there were no more to be looked into, but the very methode and order of the booke, it will sufficientlie cleare me of that first and grievousest imputation, in the point of Religion: since in the first part, where Religion is onely treated of, I speake so plainly. And what in other parts I speake of Puritanes, it is onely of their morall faults, in that part where I speake of policie: declaring when they contemne the law and so-*

veraigne

veraigné authoritie, what examplare punishment they deserve for the same. And now as to the matter it selfe where-upon this skandale is taken, that I may sufficiently satisfie all honest men, and by a just apologie raise up a brasen wall or bulwark against all the darts of the envious, I will the more narrowly rippe up the wordes, whereat they seeme to be somewhat stomacked.

First then, as to the name of Puritanes, I am not ignorant that the stile thereof doth properly belong onely to that vile sect amongst the Anabaptists, called the Familie of love; because they thinke themselves onely pure, and in a manner, without sinne, the onely true Church, and only worthie to bee participant of the Sacraments; and all the rest of the world to be but abomination in the sight of God. Of this speciall sect I principally meane, when I speake of Puritanes; divers of them, as Browne, Penrie, *and others, having at sundrie times come in Scotland, to sowe their popple amongst us (and from my heart I wish, that they had left no schollers behinde them, who by their fruites will in the owne time be manifested) and partly, indeede, I give this stile to such brainsick and headie preachers their disciples and followers, as refusing to be called of that sect, yet participates too much with their*

humours,

humours, in maintaining the above men-
tioned errours; not onely agreeing with
the generall rule of all Anabaptists, in the
contempt of the civill Magistrate, and in
leaning to their owne dreames and revelations; but particularly with this sect, in
accounting all men prophane that sweares
not to all their fantasies; in making for
everie particular question of the policie of
the Church, as great commotion, as if the
article of the Trinitie were called in controversie; in making the Scriptures to be
ruled by their conscience, and not their
conscience by the Scripture; and he that
denies the least jot of their grounds, sit
tibi tanquam ethnicus & publicanus;
not worthy to enjoy the benefite if breathing, much lesse to participate with them
of the Sacraments: and before that any of
their grounds be impugned, let King, people, law, and all be tred under foote. Such
holie warres are to be preferred to an un-
godlie peace: no, in such cases, Christian
Princes are not only to be resisted unto, but
not to be prayed for. For prayer must come
of Faith, and it is revealed to their con-
sciences, that God will heare no prayer for
such a Prince. Judge then, Christian reader, if I wrong this sort of people, in giving
them the style of that sect, whose errours
they imitate: and since they are conten-
ted to weare their liverie, let them not bee
                                    ashamed

To the Reader.

afhamed to borrowe alfo their name. It is onely of this kind of men, that in this book I write fo fharpelie; and whom I wifhe my Sonne to punifhe, in-cafe they refufe to o-bey the lawe, and will not ceafe to ftir-up a rebellion. Whom againft I have written the more bitterlie, in refpect of divers famous libels, and injurious fpeaches fpred by fome of them, not onely difhonourably in-vective againft all Chriftian Princes, but even reprochefull to our profeffion and religion, in refpect they are come out under coullour thereof: and yet were never anfwered but by Papifts, who generally meddle afwell againft them, as the religion it felfe; whereby the skandale was rather doubled, then taken away. But on the other part, I proteft upon mine honour, I meane it not generally of all Preachers, or others, that likes better of the fingle forme of policie in our Church, then of the many ceremonies in the Church of England; that are perfwaded, that their Bifhops fmels of a Papall fupremacie, that the Surplife, the cornerd Cap, and fuch like, are the outward badges of Popifh errors. No, I am fo farre from being contentious in thefe things, (which for my owne part I ever efteemed as indifferent) as I doe æqually love and honour the learned and grave men of either of thefe opinions. It can no waies become me to pronounce fo light-

ly

ly a sentence, in so olde a controversie. We all (God be praised) doe agree in the grounds, and the bitternesse of men upon such questions, doth but trouble the peace of the Church; and gives advantage and entry to the Papists by our division. But towards them, I onely use this provision, that where the Law is otherwayes, they may content themselves soberly and quietly with their owne opinions, not resisting to the authoritie, nor breaking the law of the countrie; neither above all, sturring any rebellion or schisme: but possessing their soules in peace, let them preasse by patience, and well grounded reasons, either to perswade all the rest to like of their judgements; or where they see better grounds on the other part, not to be ashamed peaceablie to incline thereunto, laying aside all preoccupied opinions.

And that this is the onely meaning of my broke, and not any coldnesse or crack in Religion, that place doth plainelie witnesse, where, after I have spoken of the faults in our Ecclesiasticall estate, I exhort my Sonne to be beneficiall unto the good men of the Ministerie; praising God there, that there is presently a sufficient number of good men of them in this kingdome: and yet are they all knowne to be against the forme of the English Church. Yea, so farre I am in that place from admitting

cor-

corruption in Religion, as I wish him in promooving them, to use such caution, as may preserve their estate from creeping to corruption; ever using that forme thorough the whole booke; where ever I speake of bad preachers, tearming them some of the ministers, and not Ministers or Ministrie in generall. And to conclude this point of Religion, what indifferencie of Religion can Momus call that in me, where, speaking of my Sonnes mariage (in case it pleased God before that time to cut the threed of my life) I plainelie forewarne him of the inconveniences that were like to insue, in case he should marrie any that be of a different profession in Religion from him: notwitstanding that the number of Princes professing our Religion bee so small, as it is hard to forcsee, how he can be that way, meetly matched according to his ranke.

And as for the other point, that by some parts in this booke, it should appeare, that I doe nourish in my minde, a vindictive resolution against England, or some principals there; it is surelie more then wonderfull unto me, upon what grounds they can have gathered such conclusions. For as upon the one part, I neither by name nor description point out England in that part of my discourse; so upon the other, I plainly bewray my meaning to be

of *Scottiſh-men, where I conclude that pur-*
poſe in theſe termes: "*That the love I*
"*beare to my Son, hath mooved me to be*
"*ſo plaine in this argument: for ſo that I*
"*diſcharge my conſcience to him in uttering*
"*the veritie, I care not what any traitour*
"*or treaſon-allower doe thinke of it.* *And*
Engliſh-men could not thereby be meant,
ſince they could be no traitors, where they
ought no alleageance. *I am not ignorant of*
a wiſe and Princely apophthegme, which the
ſame Queene of England uttered about the
time of hir owne coronation. *But the drift*
of that diſcourſe doth fully cleare my inten-
tion, being onely grounded upon that pre-
cept to my Sonne, that he ſhould not per-
mit any unreverent detracting of his prede-
ceſſors; bringing in that purpoſe of my
mother onely for an example of my experi-
ence anent Scottiſh-men, without uſing any
perſwading to him of revenge. *For a Kings*
giving of any fault the due ſtile, inſerres no
reduction of the faulters pardon. *No, I am*
by a degree nearer of kinne unto my mo-
ther then he is, neither thinke I my ſelfe,
either that unworthie, or that neere my
ende, that I neede to make ſuch a Davidi-
call *teſtament; ſince I have ever thought it*
the dutie of a worthie Prince, rather with
a pike, then a pen, to write his juſt revenge.
But in this matter I have no delight to be
large, wiſhing all men to judge of my future

pro-

instructed in, and best became me to be the informer of.

If I in this booke have beene too particularly plaine, impute it to the necessitie of the subject, not so much being ordained for the institution of a Prince in generall, as I have said, as containing particular precepts to my Sonne in speciall: whereof he could have made but a generall use, if they had not contained the particular diseases of this Kingdome, with the best remedies for the same; which it became me best as a King, having learned both the theoricke and practicke thereof, more plainely to expresse, then any simple Schoole-man, that onely knowes matters of Kingdomes by contemplation.

But if in some places it seeme too obscure, impute it to the shortnesse thereof, being both for the respect of my self, and of my Sonne, constrained thereunto: my owne respect, for fault of leasure, being so continually occupied in the affaires of my office, as my great burthen, and rest-lesse fasherie is more then knowne, to all that knowes or heares of me: for my Sonnes respect, because I know by my selfe, that a Prince so long as he is young, will be so carried away with some sorte of delight or other, that he cannot patiently abide the reading of any large volume: and when he comes to a full maturitie of age, he must be so busied

in

in the active part of his charge, as he will not bee permitted to bestow many houres upon the contemplative part thereof. So as it was neither fit for him, nor possible for mee, to have made this Treatise any more ample then it is. Indeede I am little beholden to the curiositie of some, who thinking it too large already (as appeares) for lacke of leasure to copie it, drew some notes out of it, for speeds sake; putting in the one halfe of the purpose, and leaving out the other: not unlike the man that alleadged that part of the Psalme, non est Deus; *but left out the preceding words,* Dixit insipiens in corde suo. *And of these notes, making a little pamphlet (lacking both my methode and halfe of my matter) entitled it, forsooth,* The Kings Testament: *as if I had eiked a third Testament of my owne, to the two that are in the holy Scriptures. It is true that in a place thereof, for affirmation of the purpose I am speaking of to my Sonne, I bring my selfe in there, as speaking upon my Testament: for in that sense, everie record in write of a mans opinion in any thing (in respect that papers out-lives their authors) is as it were a Testament of that mans will in that case: and in that sense it is, that in that place I call this Treatise a Testament. But from any particular sentence in a booke, to give the booke it selfe a title,*

title, is as ridiculous, as to ftile the booke of the Pfalmes, the booke of Dixit infipiens, *becaufe with thefe words one of them doth begin.*

Well, leaving thefe new baptifers and blockers of other mens books, to their owne follies, I returne to my purpofe, anent the fhortneffe of this booke: fufpecting that all my excufes for the fhortneffe thereof, fhall not fatisfie fome, efpecially in our neighbour countrie: who thought, that as I have fo narrowly in this Treatife touched all the principall ficknefles in our kingdome, with overtures for the remedies thereof, as I faid before: fo looked they to have found fomething therein, that fhould have touched the ficknefles of their ftate, in the like fort. But they will eafily excufe me thereof, if they will confider the forme I have ufed in this Treatife; wherein I onely teach my Sonne, out of my owne experience, what forme of government is fitteft for this Kingdome: and in one part thereof fpeaking of the bordours, I plainely there doe excufe my felfe, that I will fpeake nothing of the ftate of England, as a matter wherein I never had experience. I know, indeede, no Kingdome lackes her owne difeafes, and likewayes what intereft I have in the profperitie of that ftate: for although I would be filent, my blood and difcent doth fufficiently proclaime it. But notwithftanding,

To the Reader.

standing, since there is a lawfull Queene there presently raigning, who hath so long with so great wisdome and felicitie governed her Kingdomes, as (I must in true sinceritie confesse) the like hath not been read nor heard of, either in our time, or since the dayes of the Romane Emperour Augustus; it could no wayes become me, farre inferiour to her in knowledge and experience, to be a busie-bodie in other Princes matters, and to fish in other folkes waters, as the proverbe is. No, I hope by the contrarie (with Gods grace) ever to keepe that Christian rule, to doe as I would be done to: and I doubt nothing, yea even in her name I dare promise, by the by-past experience of her happie government, as I have alreadie said, that no good subject shall be more carefull to enforme her of any corruptions stollen in in her state: then she shall be zealous for the discharge of her conscience and honour, to see the same purged and restored to the auncient integritie: and further, during her time, becomes me least of any to meddle in.

And thus having resolved all the doubts, so farre as I can imagine may be mooved against this treatise; it onely rests to pray thee (charitable reader) to interpret favourably this birth of mine, according to the integritie of the author, and not looking for perfection in the worke-it selfe. As

for

for my part, I onely glorie thereof in this point, that I truſt no ſort of vertue is condemned, nor any degree of vice is allowed in it: and that (though it be not perhaps ſo gorgeruſlie decked, and richly attired as it ought to be) it is at the leaſt rightly proportioned in all the members, without any monſtrous deformitie in any of them: and ſpecially that ſince it was firſt written in ſecret, and is now publiſhed, not of ambition, but of a kind of neceſſitie; it muſt be taken of all men, for the true image of my very minde, and forme of the rule, which I have preſcribed to my ſelfe and mine. Which as in all my actions I have hitherto preaſſed to expreſſe, ſo farre as the nature of my charge, and the condition of time would permit me: ſo beareth it a diſcoverie of that, which may be looked for at my hand, and where-to, even in my ſecret thoughts, I have engaged my ſelfe for the time to come. And thus in a firme truſt, that it ſhall pleaſe God, who with my being and Crowne, gave me this mind, to maintaine and augment the ſame in me and my poſteritie, to the diſcharge of our conſcience, the maintenance of our honor, and weale of our people, I bid thee hartily fare-well.

BAΣI-

ΒΑΣΙΛΙΚΟΝ ΔΩΡΟΝ.

OF A
KING's
CHRISTIAN DUTY
Towards
GOD.

Book the First.

A S he cannot bee thought worthie
to rule and commaund others, that
cannot rule and Dantone his owne
proper affections and unreasonable appetites, so can he not be thought worthie *The true*
to governe a Christian People knowing *ground of*
and fearing God, that in his own person *good Go-*
vernment.
and heart, feareth not and loveth not the
Divine Majestie. Neither can any thing
in his Government succeed well with him,
(devise and labour as he list) as comming
from a filthie spring, if his person be un-
B sanctified:

ſanctineu. ... .u. (as that Royall Prophe

Pſa.127.1. ſaith) *Except the Lord build the houſe they labour in vain that build it : excep the Lord keepe the Citie, the keepers watcl it in vaine :* in reſpect the bleſſing of Go hath only power to give the ſucceſſe there

1 Cor.3.6. unto : and as *Paul* ſaith, he *planteth, A pollos watereth ; but it is God onely that gi veth the increaſe.* Therefore (my Sonne

Double bond of a Prince to God. firſt of all things, learne to know and lov that GOD, whome-to yee have a doubl obligation; firſt, for that hee made yo a Man ; and next, for that he made you little God to ſitte on his Throne, and rul over other men. Remember, that as i Dignitie he hath erected you above others ſo ought yee in thankfulneſſe towards him goe as farre beyond all others. A Moate i anothers eye, is a Beam into yours : a ble miſh in another, is a leaprous byle int you , and a venial ſinne (as the Papiſ call it) in another, is a great crime int

The great-nes of the fault of a Prince. you. Thinke not therefore, that the high neſſe of your dignitie diminiſheth you faults (much leſſe giveth you a licence t ſinne) but by the contrarie, your faul ſhall be aggravated, according to th height of your dignitie ; any ſinne tha yee commit, not being a ſingle ſinne, pro curing but the fall of one ; but being a exemplare ſinne , and therefore drawin with it the whole multitude to bee guilti of the fame. Remember then, that this *The true* gliftring worldlie glorie of Kings, is given *glorie of* them by God, to teach them to preffe fo *Kings.* to glifter, and fhine before their People, in al works of Sanctification and Righte-oufnes, that their Perfons as bright Lamps of Godlines and Vertue may, going in and out before their People, give light to al their fteps. Remember alfo, that by the right knowledge, and feare of God (which is *the beginning of wifedome,* as Prov.9.10. *Salomon* faith) ye fhall know all the things neceffarie for the difcharge of your dutie, both as a Chriftian, and as a King; feeing in him, as in a Mirrour, the courfe of all earthlie things, whereof he is the fpring and only moover.

Now, the onely way to bring you to *The meanes* this knowledge, is diligentlie to reade his *to know* Word, and earneftly to pray for the right *God.* underftanding thereof. *Search the Scrip* Joh.5.39. *tures,* faith Chrift, *for they beare teftimo-nie of me :* and *the whole Scripture,* faith 2 Tim. 3. Paul, *is given by infpiration of God, and* 16.17. *is profitable to teach, to convince, to correct, and to inftruct in righteoufnes ; that the man of God may be abfolute, being made perfit unto al good workes.* And moft pro-perly of any other, belongeth the reading thereof unto Kings, fince in that part of Deut.17. Scripture, where the godly Kings are firft made mention of, that were ordained to

rule

rule over the People of God, there is an expreſſe and moſt notable Exhortation and Commaundement given them, to reade and meditate in the Law of God. I joyne to this, the carefull hearing of the Doctrine with attendance and reverence: For *faith cometh by hearing,* ſaith the ſame Apoſtle. But above all, beware yee wreſt not the Wor to your owne appetite, as over many doe making it like a Bell to ſound as yee pleaſ to interpret: but by the contrarie, fram all your affections, to follow preciſely th rule there ſet down.

Rom. 10. 17.

Wherein chiefly the whole Scripture conſiſteth.

The whole Scripture chiefly containet two things: A Command, and a Prohibition; to do ſuch things, and to abſtain from the contrarie. Obey in both; ne ther thinke it enough to abſtaine fro evil, and do no good: nor thinke not th if yee doe many good things, it may ſer you for a cloake to mixe evil turnes ther with. And as in theſe two points, the who Scripture principally conſiſteth: ſo in tw degrees ſtandeth the whole Service of G by Man: interiour, or upward; exteriou or downward: The firſt, by Prayer faith towards God; the next, by work flowing therefra before the World: whi is nothing elſe, but the exerciſe of Reli on towards God, and of equitie towar your Neighbour.

Two degrees of the Service of God.

A regardable paterne.

As for the particular poynts of Religio
I nee

I neede not to dilate them; I am no hypo-
crite, follow my foote-fteppes, and your
owne prefent education therein. I thanke
God, I was never afhamed to give account
of my Profeffion, howfoever the malitious
lying Tongues of fome have traduced me:
and if my Confcience had not refolved me,
that all my Religion prefently profeffed by
me and my Kingdome, was grounded upon
the plaine wordes of the Scripture, without the which all points of Religion are
fuperfluous, as anie thing contrarie to the
fame is abomination, I had never outwardlie avowed it, for pleafure or awe of any
flefh.

And as for the points of Equitie towards
your Neighbour (becaufe that will fall in
properlie, upon the fecond part concerning
a Kings office) I leave it to the owne
roome.

For the firft part then of Mans fervice
to his God, which is Religion, that is, the *Religion.*
Worfhippe of God according to his reveal-
ed Will, it is wholie grounded upon the
Scripture, as I have alreadie fayd, quicken-
ed by faith, and conferved by Confcience.
For the Scripture, I have now fpoken of
it in generall: but that ye may the more rea-
dilie make choife of any part thereof, for
your inftruction or comfort, remember
fhortly this methode.

The whole Scripture is dited by Gods *The method*
of Scrip-
B 3   fpirit, *ture.*

spirit, thereby, as by his lively word, to inftruct and rule the whole Church Militant to the ende of the world. It is compofed of two parts, the Olde and New Teftament. The grounde of the former is the Law, which fheweth our finne, and containeth Juftice: the ground of the other is Chrift, who pardoning Sinne containeth Grace. The fumme of the Law is the Tenne Commandements, more largely dilated in the Bookes of *Mofes*, interpreted and applied by the Prophets, and by the Hiftories, are the examples fhewed of obedience or difobedience thereto, and what *præmium* or *pœna* was accordinglie given by God. But becaufe no man was able to keepe the Law, nor any part thereof, it pleafed God of his infinite wifedome and goodneffe, to incarnate his onely Sonne in our nature, for fatisfaction of his Juftice in his Suffering for us: that fince we could not be faved by Doing, we might at leaft, be faved by Beleeving.

Of the Law.

Of Grace.

The ground therefore of the word o Grace, is contained in the foure Hiftories of the birth, life, death, refurrection and afcenfion of Chrift. The larger interpretation and ufe thereof, is contained in th Epiftles of the Apoftles: and the practif in the faithfull or unfaithfull, with th Hiftorie of the Infancie and firft progreff of the Church is contained in their acts.

Woul

Would ye then know your finne by the *Vfe of the* Law? reade the bookes of *Mofes* contain- *Law.* ing it. Would yee have a commentarie thereupon? Reade the Prophets, and like-wife the bookes of the *Proverbs* and *Ec-clefiaftes*, written by that great paterne of Wifedome, *Salomon*; which will not one-ly ferve you for Inftruction, how to walke in the obedience of the Law of God, but is alfo fo full of golden Sentences, and mo-rall Precepts, in all things that can con-cerne your Converfation in the world, as among all the prophane Philofophers and Poets, ye fhall not finde fo rich a ftore-houfe of precepts of naturall Wifedome, agreeing with the will and divine wife-dome of God. Would ye fee how good men are rewarded, and wicked punifhed? Looke the hiftoricall partes of thefe fame bookes of *Mofes*, together with the Hifto-ries of *Jofua*, the *Judges*, *Ezra*, *Nehemiah*, *Efther*, and *Job*: but fpecially the bookes of the *Kings*, and *Chronicles*, wherewith ye ought to be familiarly acquainted: for there fhall ye fee your felfe, as in a Mir-rour, in the Catalogue either of the good or the evill Kings.

Would yee knowe the Doctrine, life and *Vfe of the* death of our Saviour Chrift? reade the E- *Gofpel.* vangelifts. Would ye be more particu-larly trained up in his Schoole? meditate upon the Epiftles of the Apoftles. And

would

would yee bee acquainted with the practizes of that doctrine in the perfons of the Primitive Church? Caft up the Apoftles Acts. And as to the Apocryphe bookes, I omit them, becaufe I am no Papift, as I faid before, and indeede fome of them are no wayes like the ditement of the Spirit of God.

How to reade the Scripture. But when yee reade the Scripture, reade it with a fanctified and chafte heart: admire Reverentlie fuch obfcure places as ye underftand not, blaming only your own capacitie: reade with delight the plaine places, and ftudy carefully to underftand thofe that are fomewhat difficile: preaffe to be a good textuare; for the Scripture is ever the beft interpreter of it felfe. But preaffe not curioufly to feek out farther then is contained therein; for that were over unmannerly a prefumption, to ftrive to be further upon Gods fecrets, then he hath Will ye be: for what he thought needfull for us to know, that hath he revealed there. And delight moft in reading fuch partes of the Scripture, as may beft ferve for your inftruction in your Calling; rejecting foolifh Curiofities upon Genealogies and Contentions, *which are but* *Tit. 3. 9.* *vaine and profit not,* as *Paul* faith.

Faith the nourifher of Religion. Now, as to Faith, which is the nourifher and quickner of Religion, as I have alreadie faid, it is a fyre perfwafion and apprehen-

prehenſion of the promiſes of God, apply-
ing them to your Soule: and therefore
may it juſtly be called, the Golden Chaine
that linketh the Faithfull Soule to Chriſt.
And becauſe it groweth not in our garden,
but *is the free gift of God*, as the ſame A- Philip. 1.
poſtle ſaith, it muſt be nouriſhed by Pray- 29.
er, which is nothing elſe, but a friendly
talking with God.

    As for teaching you the forme of your
prayers, the Pſalmes of *David* are the *Prayer:*
meeteſt Schoole-maſter that ye can be ac- *and whence*
to learne
quainted with (next the prayer of our Sa- *the beſt*
viour, which is the onely rule of Prayer) *forme there-*
whereout of as of moſt rich and pure Foun- *of.*
taines, yee may learne all forme of Prayer,
neceſſarie for your comfort at all occaſions.
And ſo much the fitter are they for you,
then for the common ſort, in reſpect the
Compoſer thereof was a King: and therefore beſt behooved to know a King's wants,
and what things were meeteſt to be required by a King at God's hand for remedie
thereof.

    Uſe often to pray when yee are quieteſt, *Severall*
eſpecially forget it not in your bed, how *exerciſe of*
prayer.
oft ſoever yee doe it at other times: for
publique prayer ſerveth as much for example, as for any particular comfort to the
Supplicant.

    In your Prayer, be neither over ſtraunge *What rule*
with God, like the ignorant common ſort, *or regard to*
be uſed in
                              that *prayer.*

that prayeth nothing but out of books; nor yet over homelie with him, like some of the vaine Pharisaicall Puritanes, that think they rule him upon their fingers. The former way will breed an uncouth coldnes in you towards him, the other will breede in you a contempt of him. But in hour prayer to God speake with all Reverence: For if a Subject, will not speake but reverently to a King, much lesse should any flesh presume to talke with God, as with his companion.

What to crave of God.

Crave in your Prayer, not onely things spirituall, but also things temporall, sometimes of greater, and sometimes of lesse consequence; that ye may lay up in store his grant of these things, for confirmation of your Faith, and to be an arlespenny unto you of his love. Pray, as ye finde your heart moveth you, *pro re natâ:* but see that ye sute noe unlawfull things, as revenge, lust, or such like: for that prayer cannot come of Faith: *and what-soever is done without Faith is Sinne,* as the Apostle saith.

Rom. 14. 23.

How to interpret the issue of prayer. Luk. 18.

When yee obtaine your prayer, thanke him joyfully therefore: if otherwayes, beare patiently, preassing to win him with importunitie, as the Widow did the unrighteous Judge: and if notwithstanding thereof ye be not heard, assure your selfe, God foreseeth that which yee aske is not

for

for your weale : and learne in time, fo to
interprete all the adverfities that God fhall
fend unto you; fo fhall ye in the middeft
of them, not onely be armed with patience, but joyfullie lift up your eyes from
the prefent trouble, to the happie ende
that God will turne it to.   And when ye
finde it once fo fall out by proofe, arme
your felfe with the experience thereof a-
gainft the next trouble, affuring your felfe,
though yee cannot in time of the fhowre
fee thorough the clowd, yet in the end,
fhall ye find, God fent it for your weale,
as yee found in the former.

And as for Confcience, which I called *Confcience*
the Conferver of Religion, it is nothing *the confer-*
ver of Re-
elfe, but the light of knowledge that God *ligion.*
hath planted in man, which ever watch-
ing over all his actions, as it beareth him
a joyfull teftimonie when he does right,
fo choppeth it him with a feeling that hee
hath done wrong, when ever he commit-
teth any finne.   And furely, although
this Confcience bee a great torture to the
wicked, yet it is as great comfort to the
godlie, if wee will confider it rightly. For
have we not a great advantage, that have
within our felves while we live heere, a
Count booke and Inventarie of al the *The inven-*
crimes that wee fhall be accufed of, either *tarie of ou*
life.
at the houre of our death, or at the great
day of judgement; which when wee pleafe
(yea

(yea though wee forget) will chop, and remember us to look upon it; that while we have leasure and are here, we may remember to amend; and so at the day of our triall, compeare with *new and white garments washed in the bloud of the Lambe,* as S. *John* saith, Above all then, my Sonne, labour to keepe sound this Conscience, which many prattle of, but over few feele: especially be carefull to keepe it free from two diseases, wherewith it useth oft to be infected; to wit, Leprosie, and Superstition: the former is the mother of Atheism, the other of Heresies. By a leprouse Conscience, I meane *a Cauterized Conscience,* as *Paul* calleth it, being become senselesse of Sinne, through sleeping in a carelesse Securitie, as King *Davids* was, after his Murther and Adulterie, ever till he was wakened by the Prophet *Nathans* Similitude. And by Superstition, I meane, when one restraines himselfe to any other rule in the service of God, then is warranted by the Word, the onely true Square of Gods service.

As for a preservative against this leaprosie, remember ever once in the foure and twentie houres, either in the night, or when yee are at greatest quiet, to call your selfe to account of all your last dayes actions, either wherein yee have committed things ye should not, or omitted the things

Rev.7.14.

The diseases of Conscience.

1 Tim.4.2.

Preservative against leaprosie of Conscience.

things yee fhould doe, either in your Chriftian or Kingly calling: and in that account, let not your felfe be fmoothed over
with that flattering φιλαυτία, which is o-
ver kindly a ficknes to all mankinde : but
cenfure your felfe as fharply, as if yee
were your owne enemie: *For if ye judge* 1 Cor. 11.
your felfe, ye fhall not be judged, as the 31.
Apoftle faith: and then according to your
cenfure, reforme your actions as far as ye
may ; efchewing ever, willfully and wit-
tingly to contrarie your Confcience. For
a fmall Sinne willfully committed, with
a deliberate refolution to breake the bridle
of Confcience therein, is farre more grievous before God, then a greater finne
committed in a fuddaine paffion, when
Confcience is afleepe. Remember there- *Laft ac-*
fore in all your actions, of the great Ac- *count.*
count that yee are one day to make: in
all the dayes of your life ever learning to
die, and living everie day as it were your
laft ;

> *Omnem crede diem tibi diluxiffe fupre-* Horat.lib.
>   *mum.* 1. epift.

And therefore, I would not have you to
pray with the Papifts, to bee preferved from
fuddaine death, but that God would give
you grace fo to live, as yee may everie houre
of your life be readie for death : fo fhall
ye attaine to the vertue of true Fortitude, *True For*
never being affraid for the horror of death, *titude.*

come,

come when he lift. And efpeciallie, beware to offend your Confcience, with ufe of Swearing or Lying, fuppofe but in jeft; *Foolifh ufe of oathes.* for Oathes are but an ufe, and a finne cloathed with no delight nor gaine, and therefore the more inexcufable even in the fight of men: and Lying commeth alfo much of a vile ufe, which bannifheth fhame. Therefore beware even to denie the trueth, which is a fort of lie, that may beft be efchewed by a perfon of your ranke. For if any thing bee asked at you that yee thinke not meete to reveale, if yee fay, that queftion is not pertinent for them to aske, who dare examine you further? and ufing fometimes this anfwere both in true and falfe things that fhall bee asked at you, fuch unmannerly people will never be the wifer thereof.

Againft fuperftition. And for keeping your Confcience found from that ficknes of Superftition, yee muft neither lay the fafetie of your Confcience upon the credit of your owne conceites, nor yet of other mens humours, how great Doctours of Divinitie that ever they bee: but ye muft onely ground it upon the expreffe Scripture: For Confcience not grounded upon fure knowledge, is either an ignorant fantafie, or an arrogant vanitie. Bewarre therefore in this Cafe with two extremities: the one, to beleeve with the Papifts, the Churches authoritie, better then

then your owne knowledge: the other to leane, with the Anabaptiftes, to your owne conceits and dreamed revelations.

But learne wifely to difcerne betwixt points of Salvation and indifferent things, betwixt Subftance and Ceremonies; and *Difference* betwixt the expres Commaundment and *of internall* Will of God in his Word, and the inven- *and exter-* tion or ordinance of Man: fince all that is *nall things.* neceffarie for Salvation is contained in the Scripture. For in any thing that is exprefly commanded or prohibited in the booke of God, ye cannot be over precife, even in the leaft thing; counting every finne, not according to the light eftimation, and common ufe of it in the World, but as the booke of God counteth of it. But as for all other things not contained in the Scripture, fpare not to ufe or alter them, as the neceffitie of the time fhall require. And when any of the Spiritual office-bearers in *Account of* the Church, fpeaketh unto you any thing *things ex-* that is well warranted by the Word, re- *ternall.* verence and obey them as the Heraulds of the moft high God: but, if pafling that bounds, they urge you to embrace any of their fantafies in the place of Gods Word, or would colour their particulars with a pretended zeale, acknowledge them for no other then vaine men, exceeding the bounds of their calling; and according to your office, gravely and with authori- tie redact them in order again. To

Conclusion,

To conclude then, both this purpose of Conscience, and the first part of this Booke; Keepe God more sparingly in your mouth, but aboundantly in your heart: be precise in effect, but sociall in shew: kythe more by your deedes then by your wordes the love of Vertue and hatred of Vice: and delight more to be godlie and vertuous in deed, then to be thought and called so; expecting more for your praise and reward in heaven, then heere: and apply to all your outward actions Christes commaund, to pray and give your almes secretly: So shall ye on the one part be inwardly garnished with true Christian humility, not outwardly (with the proud Pharisie) glorying in your godlines: but saying, as Christ commandeth us all, when wee have done all that wee can, *Inutiles servi sumus.* And on the other part, yee shall eschew outwardlie before the world, the suspicion of filthie proud Hypocrisie and deceitfull Dissimulation.

Luk. 17. 10.

ΒΑΣΙ-

ΒΑΣΙΛΙΚΟΝ ΔΩΡΟΝ.

OF A
KING's
DUTY
In His
OFFICE.

Book the Second.

BUt as ye are clothed with two Cal-
lings, so must ye be alike carefull
for the discharge of them both:
that as yee are a good Christian, so ye
may bee a good King, discharging your
office (as I shewed before) in the points of *The office of*
justice and equitie: which in two sundrie *a King.*
waies ye must doe: the one, in establish- *Plato in Po-*
ing and executing (which is the life of the *lit.*
law) good lawes among your people: *Isocr. in*
the other, by your behaviour in your *Synt.*
owne person, and with your servants, to

C   teach

teach your people by your example : for people are naturally inclined to counterfaite (like Apes) their Princes manners, according to the notable saying of *Plato*, expressed by the Poet,

Plato in Polit.

——————*Componitur orbis*
Regis ad exemplum, nec sic inflectere sensus
Humanos edicta valent, quàm vita regentis.

Claudian. in 4. consf. Hon.

For the part of making, and executing of lawes, consider first the true difference betwixt a lawfull good King, and an usurping Tyrant; and ye shall the more easily understand your dutie herein : for *contraria juxta se posita magis elucescunt.* The one acknowledgeth himselfe ordained for his people, having recieved from God a burthen of government whereof he must bee count-able : the other thinketh his people ordained for him, a pray to his passions and inordinate appetites, as the fruites of his magnanimitie. And therefore, as their ends are directlie contrarie, so are their whole actions, as meanes, whereby they preasse to attaine to their ends : A good King, thinking his highest honour to consist in the due discharge of his calling, employeth all his studie and paines, to procure and maintaine, by the making and execution of good lawes, the well-fare and peace of his people ; and as their naturall father

Difference of a King and a Tyrant.

Plato in Polit.

Arist. 5. Polit.

Xen. 8. Cyr. Cic. lib. 5. de Rep.

father and kindly maifter, thinketh his
greateft contentment ftandeth in their profperitie, and his greateft furetie in having
their hearts, fubjecting his owne private
affections and appetites to the weale and
ftanding of his fubjects, ever thinking the
common intereffe his chiefeft particular:
where by the contrarie, an ufurping Tyrant, thinking his greateft honour and fe-
licitie to confift in attaining *per fas, vel* *Ariſt.5.Po-lit.*
nefas, to his ambitious pretenfes, thinketh *Tacit. 4. hiſt.*
never himfelfe fure, but by the diffention
and factions among his people; and coun-
terfeiting the Saint while hee once creepe
in credit, will then (by inverting all good
lawes to ferve onely for his unrulie private
affections) frame the Common-weale ever
to advance his particular: building his
furetie upon his peoples miferie: and in
the end (as a ftep-father and an uncouth
hireling) make up his owne hand upon the ruines of the Republicke. And
according to their actions, fo receive they
their reward. For a good King (after a *The iſſue and re-wards of a good King.*
happie and famous Reigne) dieth in peace,
lamented by his Subjects, and admired by
his neighbours; and leaving a reverent
renowne behinde him in earth, obtaineth *Cic.5.de Rep.*
the crowne of eternal felicitie in heaven.
And although fome of them (which falleth
out very rarely) may bee cut off by the
treafon of fome unnaturall fubjects, yet
C 2   liveth

liveth their fame after them, and some notable plague faileth never to over-take the committers in this life, besides their infamie to all posterities hereafter. Where by the contrarie, a Tyrannes miserable and infamous life, armeth in end his owne subjects to become his burreaux: and although that rebellion be ever unlawfull on their part, yet is the world so wearied of him, that his fall is little meaned by the rest of his subjects, and but smyled at by his neighbours. And besides the infamous memorie he leaveth behinde him here, and the endlesse paine he sustaineth hereafter, it oft falleth out, that the committers not onely escape unpunished, but farther, the fact will remaine as allowed by the law in divers ages thereafter. It is easie then for you (my Sonne) to make a choyse of one of these two sorts of rulers, by following the way of vertue to establish your standing; yea, in case ye fell in the high way, yet should it be with the honourable report, and just regrate of all honest men.

The issue of Tyrannes Arist. 5. Polit. Isocr. in Sym.

And therefore to returne to my purpose anent the government of your subjects, by making and putting good lawes to execution; I remitte the making of them to your owne discretion, as yee shall finde the necessitie of new-rising corruptions to require them: for, *ex malis moribus bo-*

Anent the making of lawes.

næ

næ leges natæ funt: befides, that in this countrie, we have alreadie moe good lawes then are well execute, and am onely to infift in your forme of government anent their execution. Onlie remember, that as Parliaments have been ordained for making of lawes, fo yee abufe not their inftitution, in holding them for any mens particulars. For as a Parliament is the *The autho-* honourableft and higheft judgement in the *ritie and* land (as being the Kings heade Courte) if *Parlia-* it be well ufed, which is by making of *ments.* good lawes in it; fo is it the in-jufteft judge- *L. 12.* ment-feate that may bee, being abufed to *Tab.* mens particulars: irrevocable decreits a- gainft particular parties being given there- in under colour of generall lawes, and oft- times the Eftates not knowing themfelves whom thereby they hurt. And there- fore hold no Parliaments but for necef- fity of new lawes, which would be but feldome: for few lawes and well put in execution, are beft in a well ruled Com- mon-weale. As for the matter of fore-fal- tures, which alfo are done in Parliament, it is not good tigging with thefe things; but my advice is, ye fore-fault none but *Cic.3. de* for fuch odious crimes as may make them *leg.* unworthie ever to bee reftored againe. And *pro D. f. &* *pro Seft.* for fmaller offences, ye have other penal- ties fharpe enough to be ufed againft them.

And

Anent the execution of lawes.

And as for the execution of good lawes, whereat I left, remember that among the differences that I put betwixt the formes of the government of a good King, and an ufurping Tyrant; I fhew how a Tyrant would enter like a Saint while hee found

A juft feve- ritie to be ufed at firft.

himfelfe faft under-foote, and then would fuffer his unrulie affections to burft foorth. Therefore be ye contrarie at your firft en- trie to your Kingdome, to that *Quinquen- nium Neronis*, with his tender hearted wifh,

Sen.de cl.

Ar.7 pol.

Vellem nefcirem literas, in giving the law- full execution againft all breakers thereof but exception. For fince yee come not to your Reigne *precario*, nor by conqueft, but by right and due difcent; feare no uproares for doing of juftice, fince yee may affure your felfe, the moft part of your people

Plato 2. & 10. de Re- pub.Cie.ad Q. fr.

will ever naturallie favour juftice: provi- ding alwaies, that ye doe it onely for love to juftice, and not for fatisfying any par- ticular paffions of yours, under colour thereof: otherwife, how juftlie that ever the offender deferve it, yee are guiltie of murther before God. For ye muft confi- der, that God ever looketh to your inward intention in all your actions.

And when ye have by the feveritie of juftice once fetled your countries, and

A good mix- ture.Plato in Pol.& 9. de L. Sal. erat ad Cæ- far.

made them knowe that yee can ftrike,then may ye thereafter all the dayes of your life mixe juftice with mercie, punifhing

or

or fparing, as ye fhall finde the crime to have been wilfullie or rafhlie committed, and according to the by-paft behaviour of the committer. For if otherwife ye kyth your clemencie at the firft, the offences would foone come to fuch heapes, and the contempt of you growe fo great, that when yee would fall to punifh, the number of them to be punifhed would exceede the innocent ; and ye would be troubled to refolve whome-at to begin : and againft your nature would be compelled then to wracke manie, whom the chaftifement of fewe in the beginning might have preferved. But in this, my over-deare bought experience *A deare* may ferve you for a fufficient leffon. For *prefident.* I confeffe, where I thought (by being gracious at the beginning) to winne all mens hearts to a loving and willing obedience, I by the contrarie found, the diforder of the countrie, and the loffe of my thankes to be all my reward.

But as this fevere juftice of yours upon all offences would be but for a time, (as I have alreadie fayd) fo is there fome horrible crimes that yee are bound in confcience never to forgive: fuch as Witch-craft, *Crimes un* wilfull murther, Inceft (efpecially within *pardonable* the degrees of confanguinitie) Sodomy, Poyfoning, and falfe coyne. As for offences againft your owne perfon and authority, fince the fault concerneth your felfe, I

C 4   remit

Treason a-gainst the Prince his perfon or authoritie. remit to your owne choyfe to punifh or pardon therein, as your heart ferveth you, and according to the circumftances of the turne and the qualitie of the committer.

Here would I alfo eike another crime to be unpardonable, if I fhould not be thought partiall: but the fatherlie love I beare you, will make me breake the bounds of fhame *Stayning of* in opening it unto you. It is then, the *the blood.* falfe and unreverent writing or fpeaking of malicious men againft your Parents and Predeceffors: ye know the commaund *Exod. 20.* in Gods law, *Honour your Father and Mo-* *12.* *ther:* and confequently, fen yee are the lawfull magiftrate, fuffer not both your Princes and your Parents to be difhonour-ed by any; efpecially, fith the example *Plato 4. de* alfo toucheth your felfe, in leaving there-*Legib.* by to your fucceffors, the meafure of that which they fhall mette out againe to you in your like behalfe. I graunt we have all our faults, which, privatelie betwixt you and God, fhould ferve you for ex-amples to meditate upon, and mend in your perfon; but fhould not bee a matter of difcourfe to others whatfoever. And fith yee are come of as honourable Prede-ceffours as anie Prince living, repreffe the infolence of fuch, as under pretence to taxe a vice in the perfon, feekes craftily to ftaine the race, and to fteale the affection of the people from their pofteritie. For
how

how can they love you, that hated them whom-of ye are come? Wherefore deftroy men innocent young fucking Wolves and Foxes? but for the hatred they beare to their race: and why will a colt of a Courfer of Naples, give a greater price in a market, then an Affe-colt? but for love of the race. It is therefore a thing monftrous, to fee a man love the childe, and hate the Parents: as on the other part, the infaming and making odious of the parent, is the readieft way to bring the fonne in contempt. And for conclufion of this poynt, I may alfo alledge my owne experience. For befides the judgements of God, that with my eyes I have feene fall upon all them that were chiefe traytors to my parents, I may juftlie affirme, I never found yet a conftant byding by me in all my ftraites, by any that were of perfit age in my parents daies, but onely by fuch as conftantly bode by them. I meane fpecially by them that ferved the Queene my mother: for fo that I difcharge my confcience to you, my Sonne, in revealing to you the trueth, I care not what any traytor or treafon-allower thinke of it.

And although the crime of oppreffion *of oppref-* be not in this ranke of unpardonable crimes, *fion.* yet the over-common ufe of it in this nation, as if it were a vertue, efpecially by the greateft rank of fubjects in the land,

requireth

requireth the King to be a ſharpe cenſurer thereof. Be diligent therefore to trie, and awfull to beate downe the hornes of proude oppreſſors: embrace the quarrell of the poore and diſtreſſed, as your owne particular, thinking it your greateſt honour to repreſſe the oppreſſours: care for the pleaſure of none, neither ſpare ye any paines in your own perſon, to ſee their wrongs redreſſed: and remember of the honourable ſtile given to my grand-father of worthie memorie, in being called *the poore mans King.* And as the moſt part of a Kings office, ſtandeth in deciding that queſtion of *Meum,* and *Tuum,* among his ſubjects: ſo remember when ye ſit in judgement, that the Throne ye ſit on is Gods, as *Moſes* ſaith, and ſway neither to the right hand nor to the left; either loving the rich, or pitying the poore. Juſtice ſhould bee blinde and friendleſſe: it is not there ye ſhould reward your friends, or ſeeke to croſſe your enemies.

Heere now ſpeaking of oppreſſours and of juſtice, the purpoſe leadeth me to ſpeake of Hie-land and Bordour oppreſſions. As for the Hie-lands, I ſhortly comprehend them all in two ſorts of people: the one, that dwelleth in our maine land, that are barbarous for the moſt part, and yet mixed with ſome ſhewe of civilitie: the other that dwelleth in the Iles, and are alluterlie bar-

Ariſt. 5. Polit.
Iſocr. de reg.
Cic. in Off. & ad Q. fr.

The true glorie of Kings.

A memorable and worthie paterne.

Deut. 1.
Plato in Polit.
Cic. ad Q. frat.
Ariſt. 1. Rhet.
Pla. in Iſ.

Of the Hie-lands.

barbares, without any fort or shew of civilitie. For the first fort, put straitly to execution the lawes made alreadie by mee against their Over-lords, and the chiefes of their Clannes; and it will be no difficultie to danton them. As for the other fort, followe foorth the courfe that I have intended, in planting Colonies among them of answerable Inlands subjects, that within short time may reforme and civilize the best inclined among them: rooting out or transporting the barbarous and stubborne fort, and planting civilitie in their roomes.

But as for the Bordours, because I know, *Of the Bor-* if ye injoy not this whole Ile, according *ders.* to Gods right and your lineall difcent, ye will never get leave to brooke this North and barrenneft part thereof; no, not your owne head whereon the Crowne should stand; I neede not in that cafe trouble you with them: for then they will be the middeft of the Ile, and fo as eafily ruled as any part thereof.

And that ye may the readier with wife- *A necessarie* dome and justice governe your subjects, *point in a* by knowing what vices they are naturally *good go-* most inclined to, as a good Physician, *vernment.* who muft first know what peccant hu- *Plato in* mours his patient naturallie is most subject *Polit.* unto, before he can begin his cure, I shall therefore shortlie note unto you, the principall

cipall faults that every ranke of the people of this countrey is moft affected unto. And as for England, I will not fpeake by-geffe of them, never having beene among them ; although I hope in that God, who ever favoureth the right, before I die, to be as well acquainted with their fafhions.

As the whole fubjects of our countrey (by the auncient and foundamental policie of our Kingdome) are divided into three eftates; fo is everie eftate hereof generallie fubject to fome fpeciall vices ; which in a maner by long habitude, are thought rather vertue then vice among them: not that every particular man, in any of thefe rankes of men, is fubject unto them ; for there is good and evill of all forts : but that I meane, I have found by experience, thefe vices to have taken greateft holde with thefe rankes of men.

A confideration of the three eftates.

And firft, that I prejudge not the Church of her auncient priviledges, reafon would thee fhould have the firft place, for orders fake, in this catalogue.

The naturall fickneffes that have ever troubled, and beene the decay of all the Churches,fince the beginning of the world, chaunging the candle-fticke from one to another, as *John* faith, have beene Pride, Ambition, and Avarice : and now laft, thefe fame infirmities wrought the overthrow of the Popifh Church, in this countrey

The difeafes of the Church.

trey and divers others. But the reformation of Religion in Scotland, being extraordinarilie wrought by God, wherein many things were inordinately done by a popular tumult and rebellion, of such as blindly were doing the worke of God, but clogged with their owne passions and particular respects, as well appeared by the destruction of our policie; and not proceeding from the Princes order, as it did in our neighbour countrey of England, as likewise in Denmarke; and sundrie parts of Germanie; some firie spirited men in the Ministerie, got such a guiding of the people at that time of confusion, as finding the guste of government sweete, they begouth to fantasie to themselves, a Democratick forme of government: and having (by the iniquitie of time) been over-well baited upon the wracke, first of my Grand-mother, and next of my owne mother, and after usurping the libertie of time in my long minoritie, setled themselves so fast upon that imagined Democracie, as they fed themselves with the hope to become *Tribuni plebis:* and so in a populare government by leading the people by the nose, to beare the sway of all the rule. And for this cause, there never rose faction in the time of my minoritie, nor trouble sen-syne, but they that were upon that factious part, were ever carefull to perswade

The occasion of the Tribunate of some Puritans.

Such were the Demagogi at Athens.

and

Their formes in the State.

and allure these unrulie spirits among the Ministerie, to spouse that quarrell as their own : where-through I was ofttimes calumniated in their populare Sermons, not for any evill or vice in me, but because I was a King ; which they thought the highest evill. And because they were ashamed to professe this quarrell, they were busie to looke narrowly in all my actions ; and I warrant you a moate in my eye, yea a false report was matter enough for them to worke upon : and yet for all their cunning whereby they pretended to distinguish the lawfulnes of the office, from the vice of the person, some of them would some-

Their razing the ground of the Princely rule.

times snapper out well grosselie with the truth of their intentions : informing the people, that all Kings and Princes were naturally enemies to the libertie of the Church, and could never patiently beare the yoke of Christ : with such sound doctrine fed they their flockes. And because the learned, grave, and honest men of the Ministerie, were ever ashamed and offended with their temeritie and presumption, preassing by all good meanes by their authoritie and example, to reduce them to a greater moderation ; there could be no way found out so meet in their conceit, that were turbulent spirites among them, for maintaining their plottes, as paritie in the Church : whereby the ignorants were emboldened

emboldened (as bairdes) to crie the learn-
ed, godlie, and modeſt out of it: paritie *Their pre-*
the mother of confuſion, and enemie to *tence of Pa-*
Unitie which is the mother of ordour. For *ritie.*
if by the example thereof, once eſtabliſhed
in the Eccleſiaſticall government, the Po-
liticke and Civill eſtate ſhould be drawne
to the like, the greate confuſion that there-
upon would ariſe, may eaſily be diſcerned.
Take heed therefore (my Sonne) to ſuch *An evill*
Puritanes, verie peſtes in the Church and *ſort of ſeed-*
Common-weale: whom no deſerts can *men in the*
obliſhe, neither oathes or promiſes binde; *ſtate.*
breathing nothing but ſedition and calum-
nies, aſpiring without meaſure, rayling
without reaſon, and making their owne
imaginations (without anie warrant of the
word) the ſquare of their conſcience. I
proteſt before the great God, and ſince I
am here as upon my Teſtament, it is no
place for me to lie in, that ye ſhall never
finde with any Hie-land or Border theeves
greater ingratitude, and moe lies and vile
perjuries, then with theſe phanaticke ſpi-
rits. And ſuffer not the principals of them
to brooke your land, if ye like to ſit at
reſt: except ye would keepe them for try-
ing your patience, as *Socrates* did an evill *Xantippe.*
wife.

And for preſervative againſt their poy- *Preſerva-*
ſon, intertaine and advaunce the godlie, *tive againſt*
learned, and modeſt men of the Miniſtry, *ſuch poyſon.*
whom-

whom of (God be praifed) there lacketh
not a fufficient number: and by their provifion to Bifhopricks and Benefices (an-
nulling that vile act of Annexation, if ye
find it not done to your hand) ye fhall not

Paritie in-
compatible
with a Mo-
narchic.
onely banifh their conceited Paritie, whereof I have fpoken, and their other imagi-
narie grounds; which can neither ftand
with the ordour of the Church, nor the
peace of a Common-weale and well ruled
Monarchie: but ye fhall alfo reeftablifh
the olde inftitution of three Eftates in Parliament, which can no otherwife be done.
But in this I hope (if God fpare me daies)
to make you a faire entrie; alwaies where
I leave, follow ye my fteps.

Generall
advice in
behalfe of
the Church.
And to end my advice anent the Church
eftate, cherifh no man more then a good
Paftor, hate no man more then a proude
Puritane: thinking it one of your faireft
ftiles, to bee called a loving nourifhing-fa-
ther to the Church; feeing all the Churches
within your dominions planted with good
Paftors, the Schooles (the Seminarie of
the Church) maintained, the doctrine and
difcipline preferved in puritie, according to
Gods word, a fufficient provifion for their
fuftentation, a comelie ordour in their policie, pride punifhed, humilitie advanced,
and they fo to reverence their fuperiours,
and their flocks them, as the flourifhing
of your Church in pietie, peace, and learning

ing, may bee one of the chiefe poynts of your earthly glory: being ever alike warre with both the extremities; as well as yee represse the vaine Puritane, so not to suffer proude Papall Bishops: but as some for their qualities will deserve to bee preferred before others, so chaine them with such bonds as may preserve that estate from creeping to corruption.

The next estate now that by ordour commeth in purpose, according to their rankes in Parliament, is the Nobilitie, al- *Of the No-* though second in ranke, yet over-farre first *bilitie, and* in greatnes and power, either to do good *formes.* or evill, as they are inclined. *their*

The naturall sicknesse, that I have perceived this estate subject to in my time, hath been, a sectlesse arrogant conceit of their greatnes and power: drinking in with their verie nourismilke, that their honor stood in committing three points of iniquitie: to thrall, by oppression, the meaner sort that dwelleth neere them, to their service and following, although they hold nothing of them: to maintaine their servants and dependers in any wrong, although they be not answerable to the lawes (for any bodie will maintaine his man in a right cause) and for any displeasure, that they apprehend to bee done unto them by their neighbour, to take up a plaine feide against him; and (whithout respect of

D   God,

God, King, or Common-weale) to bang it out bravelie, he and all his kinne, a-gainſt him and all his: yea they will thinke the King farre in their common, in-caſe they agree to grant an aſſurance to a ſhort day, for keeping of the peace: where, by their naturall dutie, they are obliſhed to obey the law, and keepe the peace all the daies of their life, upon the perill of their very craigges.

Remedie of ſuch evils. Ariſt. 5. Pol.

For remeid to theſe evils in their eſtate, teach your Nobilitie to keepe your lawes as preciſely as the meaneſt: feare not their orping or being diſcontented, as long as ye rule well; for their pretended reforma-tion of Princes taketh never effect, but where evill government precedeth. Ac-

Xen. in Cyr. Iſo. in Eu. Cic. ad Q. frat.

quaint your ſelfe ſo with all the honeſt men of your Barrones and Gentlemen, and be in your giving acceſſe ſo open and affable to everie ranke of honeſt perſons, as may make them pearte without ſcarring at you, to make their owne ſutes to you them-ſelves, and not to imploy the great Lords their interceſſours; for interceſſion to Saints is papiſtry: ſo ſhall yee bring to a meaſure their monſtrous backes. And for their barbarous feides, put the lawes to due exe-cution made by me there-anent, beginning ever ratheſt at him that yee love beſt, and is moſt obliſhed unto you; to make him an example to the reſt. For ye ſhall make

all

all your reformations to begin at your el-
bowe, and so by degrees to flow to the
extremities of the land. And rest not untill
you roote out these barbarous seides, that
their effectes may bee as well smoared
downe, as their barbarous name is un-
knowne to any other nation. For if this
treatise were written eyther in French or
Latine, I could not get them named unto
you but by circumlocution. And for your
easier abolishing of them, put sharpely to
execution my Lawes made against Gunnes
and traiterous Pistolets; thinking in your
heart, terming in your speech, and using
by your punishments, all such as weare
and use them, as brigands and cut-throates.

On the other part, eschew the other extremitie, in lightlying and contemning
your Nobilitie. Remember how that errour brake the King my graundfathers
hart. But consider that vertue followeth *Pla. in 2.*
oftest noble blood: the worthinesse of their *Al. in pol.*
antecessours craveth a reverent regard to *& 5. de l.*
Arist. 2.xe
be had unto them: honour them therefore that are obedient to the law among
them, as Peers and Fathers of your land:
the more frequently that your Court can *Xen.in Cyr*
bee garnished with them, thinke it the
more your honour; acquainting and employing them in al your greatest affaires;
sen it is they must be your armes and exe-
cuters of your lawes: and so use your selfe
lovingly

lovingly to the obedient, and rigoroufly to the ftubborne, as may make the greateft of them to thinke, that the chiefeft point of their honour, ftandeth in ftriving with the meaneft of the land in humilitie towards you, and obedience to your lawes: beating ever in their ears, that one of the principall points of fervice that yee crave of them, is, in their perfons to practife, and by their power to procure due obedience to the law; without the which, no fervice they can make, can be agreeable unto you.

Of Sherif-domes and Regalities. But the greateft hinderance to the execution of our lawes in this countrie, are thefe heritable Sherif-domes and Regalities, which being in the handes of the great men, doe wracke the whole countrey. For which I know no prefent remedie, but by taking the fharper account of them in their offices; ufing all punifhment againft the flothfull, that the law will permit:

Ar.2.pol. and ever as they vaike, for any offences committed by them, difpone them never

Laudable cuftome of England. heritablie againe: preaffing, with time, to draw it to the lawdable cuftome of England: which ye may the eafilier doe, being King of both, as I hope in God ye fhall.

The third eftate. And as to the third and laft eftate, which is our Burghes (for the fmall Barrones are but an inferiour part of the Nobilitie and of their eftate) they are compofed of two

forts

sorts of men; Merchants and Crafts-men: either of these sorts being subject to their owne infirmities.

The Merchants thinke the whole Common-weale ordained for making them up; *The formes of the Merchants.* and accounting it their lawfull gaine and trade, to enrich themselves upon the losse of all the rest of the people, they transport from us things necessarie; bringing back some-times unnecessarie things, and at other times nothing at all. They buy for us the worst wares, and sell them at the dearest prices: and albeit the victuals fall or rise of their prices, according to the aboundance or skantnesse thereof; yet the prices of their wares ever rise, but never fall: being as constant in that their evill custome, as if it were a setled law for them. They are also the speciall cause of the corruption of the coyne, transporting all our owne, and bringing in forraine, upon what price they please to set on it. For order putting to them, put the good lawes in execution that are alreadie made anent these abuses: but especially do three things. Establish honest, diligent, but few searchers, for many hands make slight worke; and have an honest and diligent Treasurer to take count of them. Permit *Pla.2.de* and allure forraine Merchants to trade *Rep.8.&* here: so shall yee have best and best cheape *11.de leg.* wares, not buying them at the third hand.

D 3 And

And set every yeere down a certaine price of all things; considering first, how it is in other countries: and the price being set reasonablie downe, if the Merchants wil not bring them home on the price, crie forrainers free to bring them.

Advice a-
nent the
coyne.

And because I have made mention heere of the coyne, make your money of fine Gold and Silver; causing the people be payed with substance, and not abused with number: so shall yee enrich the Common-weale, and have a great treasure laid up in store, if yee fall in warres or in any straites. For the making it baser will breede your commoditie; but it is not to be used, but at a great necessitie.

Of Crafts-
men.
Pla.11.de
leg.

And the Craftf-men thinke, wee should be content with their worke, how bad and deere so ever it be: and if they in any thing be controlled, up goeth the blew-blanket.

A good po-
licie of Eng-
land.

But for their part take example by England, how it hath flourish-ed both in wealth and policie, since the straungers Craftf-men came in among them.

Pla.5.de
Leg.

Therefore not only permit, but allure strangers to come heere also: taking as straite order for repressing the muti-ning of ours at them, as was done in England, at their first in-bringing there.

A generall
fault in the
people.

But unto one fault, is all the common people of this Kingdome subject, as well burgh as land; which is, to judge and
speake

speake rashlie of their Prince : setting the
Common-weale upon four proppes, as wee
call it; ever wearying of the present e-
state, and desirous of novelties. For re- *Sal.in Iug.*
medie whereof (besides the execution of
lawes that are to bee used against unreverent speakers) I know no better meane,
then so to rule, as may justly stop their
mouthes, from all such idle and unreverent speeches : and so to proppe the weale
of your people, with provident care for
their good government; that justly, *Momus*
himselfe may have no ground to grudge
at: and yet so to temper and mixe your
severitie with mildnesse, that as the unjust
railers may bee restrayned with a reverent
awe; so the good and loving subjects, may
not onelie live in suretie and wealth, but
bee stirred up and invited by your benigne
curtesies, to open their mouthes in the just
praise of your so well moderated regiment.
In respect whereof, and there-with also *Ar.5.pol.*
the more to allure them to a common *Isoc. in Pa-*
amitie among themselves, certain daies *neg.*
in the yeere would bee appointed, for delighting the people with publike spectacles
of all honest games, and exercise of armes:
as also for convcening of neighbours, for
entertaining friendship and hartlinesse, by
honest feasting and merinesse. For I cannot see what greater superstition can bee
in making playes and lawfull games in May,

and good cheere at Chriſtmaſſe, then in eating fiſh in Lent, and upon Fridaies; the Papiſts as well uſing the one as the other: ſo that alwaies the Sabboths bee kept holie, and no unlawfull paſtime be uſed. And as this forme of contenting the peoples mindes, hath beene uſed in all well governed Republickes: ſo will it make you to performe in your government that old good ſentence,

Hor. de art. Poet.

Omne tulit punctum, qui miſcuit utile dulci.

Yee ſee nowe (my Sonne) howe for the zeale I beare to acquaint you with the plain and ſingle veritie of al things, I have not ſpared to be ſomthing ſatyrick, in touching wel quickly the faultes in all the eſtates of my kingdom. But I proteſt before God, I do it with the fatherly love that I owe to them all: only hating their vices, whereof there is a good number of honeſt men free in every ſtate.

And becauſe, for the better reformation of all theſe abuſes among your eſtates, it will bee a great helpe unto you, to bee well acquainted with the nature and humours of all your ſubjects, and to know particularly the eſtate of every part of your dominions; I would therefore counſell you, once in the yeare to viſit the principall parts of the country, ye ſhal be in for the time: and becauſe, I hope ye ſhall

Plut. in pol. & Min. Tac. 7. an. Mart.

be

be King of moe countries than this;
once in the three yeares to vifit all your
Kingdomes: not lipening to Vice-royes,
but hearing your felfe their complaints;
and having ordinary councels and juftice-
feats in every Kingdome, of their owne
countri-men: and the principall matters
ever to be decided by your felfe when ye
come in thofe parts.

Ye have alfo to confider, that yee muft *Protection from for-raine inju-ries.* not onely bee carefull to keepe your fubjects, from receiving any wrong of others
within; but alfo ye muft be carefull to *Xe.8.Cyr. Ar.5.pol. Polib.6. Dion.Hal. de Ro'nu.* keepe them from the wrong of any forraine Prince without: fen the fword is gi-
ven you by God, not onely to revenge
upon your owne Subjects, the wrongs
committed amongft themfelves; but further, to revenge and free them of forraine
injuries done unto them. And therefore
warres upon juft quarrels are lawfull: but
above all, let not the wrong caufe be on
your fide.

Ufe all other Princes, as your brethren, *What forms to be ufed with other Princes.* honeftly and kindly: Keepe precifely your
promife unto them, although to your
hurt: Strive with every one of them in *Ifo. in Plat. & Parag.* courtefie and thankfulnes: and as with all
men, fo efpecially with them, be plaine
and trueth-full; keeping ever that Chriftian rule, *to doe as ye would bee done to:* efpeciallie in counting rebellion againft any
other

other Prince, a crime againſt your owne ſelfe, becauſe of the preparative. Supplie not therefore, nor truſt not other Princes Rebels; but pitie and ſuccour all lawfull Princes in their troubles. But if any of them will not abſtaine, notwithſtanding what-ſoever your good deſerts, to wrong you or your ſubjects, crave redreſſe at lea-ſure; heare and doe all reaſon: and if no offer that is lawfull or honourable, can make him to abſtaine: nor repaire his wrong doing; then for laſt refuge, commit the juſtneſſe of your cauſe to God: giving firſt honeſtly up with him, and in a pub-like and honourable forme.

Ar. ad A. Varr.11.de V.P.R. Cic. 2. Off. Liu.lib.4.

Liu.lib.1. Cic. eod.

But omitting now to teach you the forme of making warres, becauſe that arte is largely treated of by many, and is bet-ter learned by practiſe then ſpeculation; I will onely ſet downe to you heere a fewe precepts therein. Let firſt the juſtneſſe of your cauſe be your greateſt ſtrength; and then omit not to uſe al lawful meanes for backing of the ſame. Conſult there-fore with no Necromancier nor falſe Pro-phet, upon the ſucceſſe of your warres; remembring on King *Saules* miſerable end: but keepe your land cleane of al South-ſayers, according to the commaund in the Law of GOD, dilated by *Jeremie.* Neither commit your quarrell to be tried by a Duell: for beſide that generally all

Of warre.

Prop.4. E-leg. Lucan.7. Varro.11. de V.P.R.

1 Sam. 31.

Deut.18.

Duell

Duell appeareth to bee un-lawfull, committing the quarrell, as it were, to a lot; whereof there is no warrant in the Scripture, since the abrogating of the olde Law; it is speciallie most un-lawfull in the person of a King: who being a publike person, hath no power therefore to dispose of himselfe, in respect, that to his preservation or fall, the safetie or wracke of the whole Common-weale is necessarily coupled, as the body is to the head. *Plut. in Sert. & Ant.*

Before ye take on warre, play the wise Kings part described by Christ; fore-seeing how yee may beare it out with all necessarie provision: especially remember, that money is *Nervus belli*, Choose olde experimented Captaines, and yoong able Souldiers. Be extreamely straite and severe in Martiall Discipline, as well for keeping of order, which is as requisit as hardinesse in the wars, and punishing of slouth, which at a time may put the whole Armie in hazard; as likewise for repressing of mutinies which in Warres are wonderfull daungerous. And looke to the Spaniard, whose great successe in all his warres, hath onely come through straitnesse of Discipline and order: for such errours may bee committed in the warres, as cannot bee gotten mended againe. *Luke 14.* *Thuc. 2. Sal. in Iug. Cic.pro l. Man. Demost. olyn. 2. Liu.li.30. Veget.1. Cæs.1.& 3. de bel.civili Prob. in Thras.*

Be in your owne person walkrife, diligent, and painfull; using the advice of
such

Cæſ.1.de
Bello ciu.
Liu.l.7.
Xen.1.&
5.Cyr.& de
diſcip.mi.

Xen. in
Ageſ.
Pol.l.5.

Xen.1.Cyr.
Thuc.5.

Iſoc. ad
Phil.
Pla. 9. de
leg.
Liu.l.22.
& 31.
Tac.2.hiſ.
Plut. de
fort.

Of peace.
Iſocr. in
Arch.

Polib.3.
Cic.1.Off.
& 7. Phil.
Tac.4.hiſ.

ſuch as are skilfulleſt in the craft, as yee muſt alſo doe in all other. Be homely with your Souldiers as your companions, for winning their harts, and extreamely liberall, for then is no time of ſparing. Be colde and fore-feeing in deviſing, conſtant in your reſolutions, and forward and quicke in your executions. Fortifie well your Campe, and aſſaile not raſhly without an advantage: neither feare not lightly your enemie. Be curious in deviſing Stratagems, but alwaies honeſtly: for of any thing they worke greateſt effects in the warres, if ſecrecie be joined to invention. And once or twice in your owne perſon hazard your ſelfe fairely; but, having acquired ſo the fame of courage and magnanimitie, make not a dailie Souldier of your ſelfe, expoſing raſhly your perſon to every perill: but conſerve your ſelfe thereafter for the weale of your people; for whoſe ſake ye muſt more care for your ſelfe, then for your owne.

And as I have counſelled you to be ſlow in taking on a warre; ſo adviſe I you to be ſlow in peace-making. Before ye agree, looke that the ground of your warres be ſatisfied in your peace; and that ye ſee a good ſuretie for you and your people: otherwaies, a honorable and juſt warre is more tolerable, than a diſhonourable and diſadvantageous peace.

But

But it is not enough to a good King, by
the fcepter of good lawes well execute to
governe, and by force of armes to protect
his people; if he joyne not therewith his
vertuous life in his owne perfon, and in
the perfon of his Court and companie: by
good example alluring his fubjects to the
love of vertue, and hatred of vice.   And
therefore (my Sonne) fith all people are *A Kings*
naturally inclined to followe their Princes *life muft be*
example (as I fhewed you before) let it *exemplare.*
not be faid, that ye commaund others to *Pla.in Pol.*
keep the contrarie courfe to that, which *& 4.de leg.*
in your owne perfon yee practife: making
fo your wordes and deeds to fight together:
but by the contrarie, let your owne life
be a law-book and a mirrour to your people; that therein they may read the practife of their owne lawes; and therein
they may fee, by your image, what life
they fhould leade.

And this example in your owne life and
perfon, I likewife devide in two parts:
The firft, in the governement of your
Court and followers, in all godlineffe and
vertue: the next, in having your minde
decked and enriched fo with all vertuous
qualities, that there-with ye may worthi-
lie rule your people.   For it is not enough *Plato in*
that ye have and retaine (as prifoners) *Thea. &*
within your felfe never fo many good qua- *Euth.*
lities and vertues, except ye imploy them,

and

and fet them on worke, for the weale of them that are committed to your charge: *Virtutis enim laus omnis in actione confiftit.*

Ar.1.Eth. Cic. in Off.

Firft then, as to the governement of your Court and followers; King *David* fets downthe beft precepts, that any wife and Criftian King can practife in that point. For as ye ought to have a great care for the ruling wel of all your fubjects: fo ought ye to have a double care for the ruling well of your owne fervants; fince unto them ye are both a Politike and Oeconomick governour. And as every one of the people will delight to follow the example of any of the Courteours, as well in evill as in good: fo what crime fo horrible can there be committed and over-feen in a Courteour, that will not be an exemplare excufe for any other boldly to commit the like? And therefore in two points have yee to take good heede anent your Court and houfehold. Firft, in choofing them wifely: next, in carefully ruling them whom yee have chofen.

Of the Court. Pfal.101.

Cic.ad Q. frat.

It is an olde and true faying, that a kindlie Auer will never become a good horfe: for albeit good education and companie be great helps to Nature, and education be therefore moft juftly called *altera natura:* yet is it evill to get out of the flefh, that is bred in the bone, as the olde proverbe faith. Be verie warie then in making choife

Pla.5. de leg. Ar.2.œc.

choife of your fervants and companie;———*Nam*

Ovid.5.de Trift.

> *Turpius ejicitur, quam non admittitur*
> *hofpes :*

and many refpects may lawfullie let an ad-
miffion, that will not be fufficient caufes
of deprivation.

All your fervants and Court muft be
compofed partly of minors, fuch as young
Lords, to be brought up in your companie, or Pages and fuch like; and partly of
men of perfite age, for ferving you in fuch
roomes, ought to bee filled with men of
wifedome and difcretion. For the firft
forte, yee can doe no more, but choofe
them within age, that are come of a good
and vertuous kinde, *In fide parentum*, as
Baptifme is ufed. For though *anima non*
venit ex traduce, but is immediatelie crea-
ted by GOD, and infufed from above :
yet it is moft certaine, that vertue or vice
will oftentimes, with the heritage, be
transferred from the parents to the pofteritie, and runne on a blood (as the proverbe is) the fickneffe of the mind be-
comming as kindly to fome races, as thefe
ficknefles of the bodie, that infects in the
feede. Efpecially choofe fuch minors, as
are come of a true and honeft race, and
have not had the houfe whereof they are
defcended, infected with falfehood.

Of the choife of fervants.

Ar.1.& 5. pol. Cic.ad Q. frat.

Witneffe the experi- ence of the late houfe of Gowrie.

Pla.6.de Leg. Ar.2.æc. & 1.pol.

And

And as for the other fort of your companie and fervantes, that ought to bee of perfect age: firft, fee that they be of a good fame, and without blemifh: otherwife, what can the people thinke, but that ye have chofen a companie unto you, according to your own humour, and fo have preferred thefe men, for the love of their vices and crimes, that yee knew them to bee guiltie of? For the people that fee you not within, cannot judge of you, but according to the outwarde appearance of your actions and companie; which onely is fubject to their fight. And next, fee that they be indued with fuch honeft qualities, as are meete for fuch offices, as yee ordaine them to ferve in; that your judgement may bee knowne in imploying every man according to his gifts. And fhortly, follow good King *Davids* counfell in the choife of your fervants, by fetting your eyes upon the faithfull and upright of the land to dwell with you.

But heere I muft not forget to remember, and according to my fatherly authoritie, to charge you to preferre fpecially to your fervice, fo many as have truely ferved me, and are able for it: the reft, honorably to reward them, preferring their pofteritie before others, as kindlieft: fo fhall ye not only be beft ferved, (for if the haters of your parents cannot love you,

Pla.6.de Leg.
Ifoc.in Pan.
Ar.5.Pol.

Dem.2.Ph.

Plat.7.de Rep.3.&
12.de L.
Arift.5.&
6. Pol.

Pfal.101.

A tranfmiffion of hereditary kindneffe.

as

as I shewed before, it followeth of necessitie their lovers must love you) but further, ye shall kyth your thankfull memorie of your father, and procure the blessing of these old servants, in not missing their old maister in you; which otherwayes would be turned in a prayer for me, and a curse for you. Use them therefore when God shall call me, as the testimonies of your affection towards me: trusting and advancing those farthest, whom I found faithfullest: which ye must not discerne by their rewards at my hand (for rewards, as they are called *Bona fortunæ*, so are they subject unto fortune) but according to the trust I gave them; having oft-times had better hart then hap to the rewarding of sundry. And on the other part, as I wish you to kyth your constant love towards them that I loved; so I desire you to kyth in the same measure, your constant hatred to them that I hated: I meane, bring not home, nor restore not such as yee finde standing banished or forefaulted by me. The contrarie would kyth in you over great a contempt of me, and lightnesse in your owne nature: for how can they bee true to the Sonne, that were false to the Father?

But to returne to the purpose anent the choyse of your servants, ye shall by this wise forme of doing, eschew the inconvenients, that in my minoritie I fell in, anent

E   the

the choife of my fervants. For by them that had the commaund where I was brought up, were my fervants put unto mee; not choofing them that were meeteft to ferve me, but whom they thought meeteft to ferve their turne about me; as kythed well in many of them at the firft rebellion raifed againft me: which compelled mee to make a great alteration among my fervants. And yet the example of that corruption, made mee to bee long troubled there after with foliciters, recommending fervants unto me more for ferving in effect, their friends that put them in, then their mafter that admitted them. Let my example then teach you to follow the rules heere fet downe: choofing your fervants for your owne ufe, and not for the ufe of others. And fince yee muft be *communis parens* to all your people, fo choofe your fervants indifferentlie out of all quarters; not refpecting other mens appetites, but their owne qualities. For as ye muft commaund all, fo reafon would, ye fhould be ferved out of all, as yee pleafe to make choife.

But fpeciallie take good heede to the choife of your fervants, that ye preferre to the offices of the crowne and eftate: for in other offices ye have onely to take heede to your owne weale; but thefe concerne likewife the weale of your people;

for

A dome- ftick and neere example.

Ar.2.pol.

Of the officers of the crowne. Pl.3.de Rep. Cic. ad Q. frat. Ifoc. in for the which yee muſt bee anſwer-able *Panath. ad* to God. Chooſe then for all theſe offices, *Nic. & de* men of knowne wiſdome, honeſtie, and *pace.* *Thuc.6.* good conſcience; well practiſed in the *Plut. in* points of the crafte, that ye ordaine them *pol.* for; and free of all factions and partiali- ties: but ſpeciallie free of that filthy vice *Plato in* of Flattery, the peſt of all Princes, and *Phedr.& Menex.* wrack of Republickes. For ſince in the firſt part of this treatiſe, I for-warned you *Ar. 5.pol.* to be warre with your owne inward flat- *Iſ. in Sym.* terer φιλαυτια, how much more ſhould yee *Tac.3.hiſ. curt.8.* bee warre with outward flatterers, who are nothing ſo ſib to you, as your ſelfe is; by the ſelling of ſuch counterfeit wares, onely preaſſing to ground their greatneſſe upon your ruines? And therefore be care- full to preferre none, as ye will be anſwer- able to God, but onely for their worthi- neſſe. But ſpecially chooſe honeſt, dili- *Of publike* gent, meane, but reſponſall men, to be *receivers.* your receivers in money matters: meane I ſay, that yee may when ye pleaſe, take a ſharpe account of their intromiſſion, without perill of their breeding any trou- ble to your eſtate: for this over-ſight hath beene the greateſt cauſe of my miſ-thri- ving in money matters. Eſpecially, put *A ſpeciall* never a forrainer, in any principall office *principle in policie.* of eſtate: for that will never faile to ſtirre *Ar.5.pol.* up ſedition and envie in the countrie-mens *Cic. ad Q. frat.* hearts, both againſt you and him. But

E 2   (as

(as I faid before) if God provide you with moe countries then this, choofe the borne-men of every countrey, to bee your chiefe counfellers therein.

And for conclufion of my advice anent the choife of your fervants, delight to be ferved with men of the nobleft blood that may be had : for befides that their fervice fhall breede you great good-will and leaft envy, contrary to that of ftart-ups ; ye fhall oft finde vertue followe noble races, as I have fayd before fpeaking of the No-bilitie.

Pl.in 1.
Al. in pol.
& 5. de l.
Ar.2.œc.

Nowe, as to the other poynt, anent your governing of your fervants when yee have chofen them ; make your Court and companie to be a paterne of Godlineffe and all honeft vertues, to all the reft of the people. Be a dayly watch-man over your fervants, that they obey your lawes præcifelie : for how can your lawes bee kept in the countrie, if they be broken at your eare? Punifhing the breach thereof in a Courteour, more feverely, than in the perfon of any other of your fubjeĉts : and above all, fuffer none of them (by abufing their credite with you) to oppreffe or wrong any of your fubjeĉtes. Bee home-lie or ftrange with them, as yee think their behaviour deferveth, and their na-ture may beare with. Thinke a quarrel-lous man a peft in your companie. Bee carefull

Governe-
ment of the
court.
Ifoc. in
Areop.

Id. in Pa-
nath.

Ar.2.pol.

Tac.1.hif.

carefull ever to preferre the gentileſt na- *Val.l.2.*
tured and truſtieſt, to the inwardeſt offi- *Curt.4.*
ces about you; eſpecially in your chalmer.
Suffer none about you to medle in any *Dem.oſt.*
mens particulars; but like the Turkes Ja- *8. phil.*
Sal. in Cat.
niſares, let them knowe no Father but *Liu.22.*
you, nor particular but yours. And if
any wil medle in their kin or friends quar-
relles, give them their leave: for ſince ye
muſt bee of no ſurname nor kinne, but
æquall to all honeſt men; it becometh
you not to be followed with partiall or
factious ſervants. Teach obedience to
your ſervantes, and not to thinke them- *Tac. eod.*
ſelves over-wiſe: and, as when any of *& 1. An.*
them deſerveth it, yee muſt not ſpare to
put them away; ſo, without a ſcene cauſe *The*
change none of them. Pay them, as all *ground-*
ſtone of
others your ſubjects, with *præmium* or *good go-*
pæna, as they deſerve; which is the very *vernment.*
ground-ſtone of good governement. Em- *Ar.5.po.*
Ta. in Ag.
ploy every man as yee thinke him quali- *Dio l.l.52.*
fied, but uſe not one in all things, leaſt
he waxe proud, and be envyed by his fel- *Xen. in A-*
lowes. Love them beſt, that are plain- *geſ.*
Iſ. in Sym.
neſt with you, and diſguiſe not the truth *& ad Ph.*
for all their kinne: ſuffer none to bee evill *Id. de per-*
mutat.
tongued, nor backbiters of them they *Cic. ad Q.*
hate: commaund a hartly and brotherly *frat.*
love among all them that ſerve you. And
ſhortly, maintaine peace in your Court,
banniſh envie, cheriſh modeſtie, banniſh
deboſhed

deboshed infolence, fofter humilitie, and repreffe pride : fetting downe fuch a comely and honorable order in all the points of your fervice ; that when ftrangers fhal vifit your Court, they may with the 1 King.10. Queene of *Sheba*, admire your wifdome in the glory of your houfe, and comely order among your fervants.

Of mariage. But the principall bleffing that ye can get of good companie, will ftand in your marying of a godly and vertuous wife : for fhee muft be nearer unto you, then Gen.2.23. any other companie, being *Flefh of your flefh, and bone of your bone*, as *Adam* faid of *Hevah*. And becaufe I know not but God may call me, before ye be readie for mariage ; I will fhortly fet downe to you here my advice therein.

 Firft of all confider, that mariage is the greateft earthly felicite or miferie, that can come to a man, according as it pleafeth God to bleffe or curffe the fame. Since then without the bleffing of GOD, yee cannot looke for a happie fucceffe in mari-*Preparati-* age : ye muft be carefull both in your pre-*on to mari-* paration for it, and in the choyfe and ufage *age.* of your wife, to procure the fame. By your preparation, I meane, that ye muft keepe your bodie cleane and unpolluted, till yee give it to your wife ; whome-to onely it belongeth. For how can yee juftlie crave to bee joyned with a pure

Virgine,

Virgine, if your body be polluted ? Why
ſhould the one halfe be cleane, and the
other defiled ? And although I know, Fornication is thought but a light and a veniall
ſin, by moſt part of the world; yet remember well what I ſaid to you in my
firſt booke anent conſcience : and count
everie ſinne and breach of Gods lawe, not
according as the vaine world eſteemeth of
it; but as God the judge and maker of the
lawe accounteth of the ſame. Heare
God commaunding by the mouth of *Paule*,
to *abſtaine from Fornication*, declaring that
the *Fornicator ſhall not inherit the kingdome of heaven:* and by the mouth of *John*,
reckoning out Fornication amongſt other
grievous ſinnes, that debarres the committers amongſt *Dogges and ſwine, from entrie in that ſpirituall and heavenlie Jeru-
ſalem.* And conſider, if a man ſhall once
take upon him, to count that light, which
God calleth heavie; and veniall that ,
which God calleth grievous ; beginning
firſt to meaſure any one ſinne by the rule
of his luſt and appetites, and not of his
conſcience ; what ſhall let him to doe ſo
with the next, that his affeċtions ſhall
ſtirre him to, the like reaſon ſerving for
all : and ſo to goe forward till he place
his whole corrupted affeċtions in Gods
roome ? And then what ſhall come of him ;
but, as a man given over to his owne fil-

1 Cor.6.
10.

Rev.22.
15.

*The dange-
rous effeċts
of luſt.*

E 4   thie

thie affections, fhall perifh into them?
And becaufe wee are all of that nature,
that fibbeft examples touches us neereft,
confider the difference of fucceffe that God
granted in the Mariages of the King my
grand-father, and mee your owne father:
the reward of his incontinencie (proceeding from his evill education) being the
fuddaine death at one time, of two pleafant young Princes; and a daughter only
borne to fucceede to him, whom hee had
never the hap, fo much as once to fee or
bleffe before his death: leaving a double
curfe behinde him to the land, both a
woman of fexe, and a new borne babe of
age to raigne over them. And as for the
bleffing God hath beftowed on me, in
graunting me both a greater continencie,
and the fruits following there-upon; your
felfe, and fib folkes to you, are (praife be
to God) fufficient witneffes: which, I
hope the fame God of his infinite mercy,
fhall continue and increafe, without re-
pentance to me and my pofteritie. Be not
afhamed then, to keep cleane your bodie,
which is the Temple of the holy Spirit,
notwithftanding all vaine allurements to
the contrarie: difcerning truly and wifely
of every vertue and vice, according to the
true qualities thereof; and not according
to the vaine conceits of men.

As for your choife in Mariage, refpect
chiefly

A dome-ſticke ex-ample.

1 Cor. 6. 19.

chiefly the three caufes, wherefore Mariage was firft ordained by God: and then joyne three acceffories, fo farre as they may be obtained, not derogating to the principals.

The three caufes it was ordained for, *Mariage* are, for ftaying of luft, for procreation of *ordained* children, and that man fhould by his wife *caufes.* get a helper like himfelfe. Deferre not *Ar.7.pol.* then to marrie till your age; for it is or- dained for quenching the luft of your youth. Efpeciallie a King muft tymouflie marrie for the weale of his people. Nei- ther marrie ye, for any acceflorie caufe or *Id.eod.* worldly refpects, a woman un-able, ei- ther through age, nature, or accident, for procreation of children: for in a King that were a double fault, afwel againft his owne weale, as againft the weale of his people. Neither alfo marrie one of knowne evill conditions, or vicious education: for the woman is ordained to bee a helper, and not a hinderer to man.

The three acceffories, which (as I have *Acceflorie* faid) ought alfo to be refpected, without *caufes of* derogating to the principall caufes, are *Æg.Ro.2.* beautie, riches, and friendfhip by alliance, *de reg.pr.* which are all bleffings of God. For beau- tie increafeth your love to your wife, con- tenting you the better with her, without caring for others: and riches and great al- liance, doe both make her the abler to bee a helper unto you. But if, over great

refpect

respect being had to these accessories, the principall causes be over-seene (which is over oft practised in the world) as of themselves they are a blessing being well used: so the abuse of them will turne them in a curse. For what can all these worldly respects availe, when a man shall find himselfe coupled with a Devill, to be one flesh with him, and the halfe marrow in his bed? Then (though too late) shall hee finde that beautie without bountie, wealth without wisdome, and great friendship without grace and honestie; are but faire shewes, and the deceitfull masques of infinite miseries.

But have ye respect, my Sonne, to these three speciall causes in your Mariage, which flow from the first institution thereof, & *cætera omnia adjicientur vobis*, And therefore I would rathest have you to marrie one that were fully of your owne Religion; her ranke and other qualities being agreeable to your estate. For although that to my great regrate, the number of any Princes of power and account, professing our Religion, be but very small; and that therefore this advice seemes to be the more straite and difficile: yet ye have deepely to weigh and consider upon these doubts, how ye and your wife can be of one flesh, and keepe unitie betwixt you, beeing members of two opposite Chuches:

Matth. 6. 33. A speciall caution in mariage.

dis-

disagreement in Religion bringeth ever with it, disagreement in manners; and the dissention betwixt your Preachers and hers, will breede and foster a dissention among your subjects, taking their example from your familie; besides the perill of the evill education of your children. Neither pride you that yee will be able to frame and make her as ye please: that deceived *Salomon* the wisest King that ever was: the grace of perseverance not being a flower that groweth in our garden.

Remember also that mariage is one of the greatest actions that a man doth in all his time, especially in taking of his first wife: and if hee marrie first basely beneath his ranke, he will never be the lesse accounted of there-after. And lastlie, remember *For keeping the blood pure.* to choose your wife as I advised you to choose your servants: that she be of a *Pla.5. de Rep.* whole and cleane race, not subject to the hereditarie sicknesses, either of the soule or the body. For if a man will be care- *Cic.2.de Diu.* full to breed horses and dogs of good *Arist.de gen. An.* kindes; how much more carefull should *Lucr.4.* hee be, for the breede of his owne loynes? So shall ye in your mariage have respect to your conscience, honour, and naturall weale in your successours.

When yee are married, keepe inviolablie your promise made to God in your mariage; which standeth all in doing of

one

one thing, and abftaining from another : to
treate her in all things as your wife and the
halfe of your felfe; and to make your bodie
(which then is no more yours, but properly
hers) common with none other.   I truft I
neede not to infift here to diffwade you
from the filthie vice of adulterie: remember onely what folemne promife ye make
to God at your marriage : and fince it is
only by the force of that promife that your
children fucceed to you, which otherwayes they could not doe; equitie and
reafon would, yee fhould keepe your part
thereof.   God is ever a fevere avenger of
all perjuries; and it is no oath made in jeft,
that giveth power to children to fucceede
to great Kingdomes.   Have the King my
Grand-fathers example before your eyes,
who by his adulterie, bred the wrack of
his lawfull daughter and heire; in beget-
ting that baftard, who unnaturally re-
belled, and procured the ruine of his owne
Soveraigne and fifter.   And what good
her pofteritie hath gotten fen-fyne, of fome
of that unlawfull generation, *Bothuell* his
treacherous attempts can beare witneffe.
Keepe precifely then your promife made at
mariage, as ye would wifh to bee parta-
ker of the bleffing therein.

And for your behaviour to your wife,
the Scripture can beft give you counfell
therein.   Treate her as your owne flefh,
com-

Pla.11.de leg.
If.in Sym.

Cic.2.de leg.

commaund her as her Lord, cherish her
as your helper, rule her as your pupill,
and please her in all things reasonable; but
teach her not to be curious in things that *Arist.8.*
belonges her not.   Ye are the head, she is *Æth. & 1.*
your body: It is your office to commaund, *Pol.*
and hers to obey; but yet with such a *Arist. in*
sweete harmonie, as shee should be as rea- *œco.*
die to obey, as yee to commaunde; as
willing to followe, as ye to go before:
your love beeing wholie knit unto her,
and all her affections lovingly bent to followe your will.

   And to conclude, keepe specially three
rules with your Wife: first, suffer her ne- *Ar. 1.*
ver to medle with the politick government *Rhet.*
of the common-weale, but hold her at *Pl. in Me-*
the Oeconomick rule of the house; and *non.*
yet all to be subject to your direction: *Ægid.R.*
keepe carefullie good and chaste companie *de reg. pr.*
about her; for women are the frailest sexe: *Pl. 5. de*
and bee never both angrie at once; but *Rep. & 7.*
when yee see her in passion, ye should with *de leg.*
reason danton yours.   For both when yee
are setled, ye are meetest to judge of her
errours; and when shee is come to her
selfe, shee may be best made to apprehend
her offence, and reverence your rebuke.

   If God send you succession, bee carefull *A Kings*
for their vertuous education: love them *behaviour*
as yee ought, but let them knowe as much *towards*
of it, as the gentlenesse of their nature *his chil-*
dren.
                                   will

Pl. in The.
4. & 5. de
Rep. & 6.
& 7. de l.
Ar. 7. pol.

A caution
for eschew-
ing future
division.

will deſerve ; contayning them ever in a reverent love and feare of you.   And in caſe it pleaſe God to provide you to all theſe three kingdomes, make your eldeſt ſonne *Iſaac*, leaving him all your king-domes ; and provide the reſt with private poſſeſſions.   Otherwaies by dividing your kingdomes, ye ſhall leave the ſeede of di-viſion and diſcorde among your poſteritie: as befell to this Ile , by the diviſion and aſſignement thereof, to the three ſonnes of

Poli.l.1.

Crownes
comes not
in com-
merce.

Brutus, *Locrine* , *Albanact*, and *Camber*. But if God give you not ſucceſſion, defraud never the neareſt by right, what-ſo-ever conceit yee have of the perſon. For King-domes are ever at Gods diſpoſition, and in that caſe we are but live-rentars, lying no more in the Kings, nor peoples hand to diſpoſſeſſe the righteous heire.

And as your company ſhould bee a pa-terne to the reſt of the people, ſo ſhould your perſon bee a lampe and mirrour to your companie : giving light to your ſer-vantes to walke in the path of vertue, and repreſenting unto them ſuch worthie qua-lities, as they ſhould preaſſe to imitate.

Pl. in Pol.
Cic. ad
Q. frat.

The right
uſe of tem-
perance.
Ar. 5. pol.
Pol. 6.
Cic. 1. of.
2. de inven.
& in Par.

I neede not to trouble you with the par-ticular diſcourſe of the foure Cardinall ver-tues, it is ſo troden a path: but I will ſhortly ſay unto you; make one of them, which is Temperance, Queene of all the reſt within you.   I meane not by the

vulgar

vulgar interpretation of Temperance, which only confifts in *guftu & tactu*, by the moderating of thefe two fenfes: but I meane of that wife moderation, that firft commanding your felfe, fhall as a Queene, commaund all the affections and paffions of your minde; and, as a Phyficion, wifely mixe all your actions according thereto. Therefore, not onely in all your affections and paffions, but even in your moft vertuous actions, make ever moderation to bee the chiefe ruler. For although holineffe bee the firft and moft requifite qualitie of a Chriftian, as proceeding from a feeling feare and true knowledge of God: yet yee remember how in the conclufion of my firft booke, I advifed you to moderate all your outwarde actions flowing there-fra. The like fay I now of Juftice, which is the greateft vertue, that properly belongeth to a Kings office.

In Holineffe.

Ufe Juftice, but with fuch moderation, as it turne not in Tyrannie: otherwaies *fummum jus*, is *fumma injuria*. As for example: if a man of a knowne honeft life, be invaded by brigandes or theeves for his purfe, and in his owne defence flaie one of them, they being both moe in number, and alfo knowne to be deboshed and infolent livers; whereby the contrarie, hee was fingle alone, beeing a man of founde reputation: yet becaufe they were not at the

In Juftice.
Pl. 4. de leg.
Ar. 1. mag. mor.
Cic. 1. of. pro Rab. & ad Q. f. Sen. de cl.

the horne, or there was no eie-witneſſe preſent that could verifie their firſt invading of him; ſhall hee therefore loſe his head? And likewiſe, by the lawe-burrowes in our lawes, men are prohibited under great pecuniall paines, from any waies invading or moleſting their neighbours perſon or bounds: if then his horſe breake the halter, and paſtor in his neighbours medowe, ſhall he pay two or three thouſand pounds, for the wantonneſſe of his horſe, or the weakneſſe of his halter? Surelie no. For lawes are ordained as rules of vertuous and ſociall living, and not to be ſnares to trap your good ſubjects: and therefore the law muſt bee interpreted according to the meaning, and not to the literall ſenſe thereof: *Nam ratio eſt anima legis.*

Ar. 5. æth. & 5. rhet. Cic. pro Cæc.

And as I ſaid of Juſtice, ſo ſay I of Clemencie, Magnanimitie, Liberalitie, Conſtancie, Humilitie, and all other Princelie vertues; *Nam in medio ſtat virtus.* And it is but the craft of the Devill that falſelie coloureth the two vices that are on either ſide thereof, with the borrowed titles of it, albeit in verie deede they have no affinitie therewith: and the two extremities themſelves, although they ſeeme contrarie, yet growing to the height, runnes ever both in one. For *in infinitis omnia concurrunt*; and what difference is betwixt

The falſe ſemblance of extremities.

Their coincidence.

betwixt extreame tyrannie, delighting to deſtroy all mankinde; and extreame ſlackneſſe of puniſhment, permitting every man to tyrannize over his companion? Or what differeth extreame prodigalitie, by waſting of all to poſſeſſe nothing; from extreame niggardneſſe, by hoarding up all to enjoy nothing; like the Aſſe that carrying victuall on her backe, is like to ſtarve for hunger, and will bee glad of thiſtles for her part? And what is betwixt the pride of a glorious *Nebuchadnezzar,* and the prepoſterous humilitie of one of the proude Puritanes, clayming to their paritie, and crying, We are all but vile wormes; and yet will judge and give lawe to their King, but will bee judged nor controlled by none? Surelie, there is more pride under ſuch a ones blacke bonnet, then under *Alexander* the great his Diademe,as was ſaid of *Diogenes* in the like caſe.

But above all vertues, ſtudie to know well your owne craft, which is to rule your people. And when I ſay this, I bid you knowe all crafts. For except yee knowe everie one, how can yee controule everie one, which is your proper office? Therefore beſides your education, it is neceſſarie ye delight in reading, and ſeeking the knowledge of all lawfull things; but with theſe two reſtrictions: firſt, that ye chooſe idle houres for it, not

The right extention of a Kings craft.

*Plat.in Pol.
5.de Rep.
& epiſt.7.
Cic.ad Q:
frat. &
de or.*

F   inter-

interrupting therewith the difcharge of your office: and next, that ye ftudie not *Id.1.de fin.* for knowledge nakedly; but that your principall end bee, to make you able thereby to ufe your office; practifing according to your knowledge in all the poynts of your calling: not like thefe vaine Aftrologians, that ftudie night and *Id. 1.Of.* day on the courfe of the ftarres, onely that they may, for fatisfying their curiofitie, knowe their courfe. But fince all Artes and Sciences are linked everie one with other, their greateft principles agreeing in one (which mooved the Poets to faine the nine Mufes to bee all fifters) ftudie them, that out of their harmonie, yee may fucke the knowledge of all faculties; and confequently, be on the counfell of all crafts, that yee may be able to containe them all in order, as I have alreadie faid. For knowledge and learning is a light burthen, the weigh thereof will never preffe your fhoulders.

The Scripture. *Deut.*17.   Firft of all then, ftudie to be well feene in the Scriptures, as I remembred you in the firft booke; afwell for the knowledge of your owne falvation, as that ye may bee able to containe your Church in their calling, as *Cuftos utriufque Tabulæ.* For the ruling them well, is no fmall point of your office; taking fpeciallie heede, that they vague not from their text in the
Pulpit:

Pulpit: and if ever yee would have peace in your land, fuffer them not to meddle in that place with the eftate or policie: but punifh feverely the firft that prefumeeth to it. Doe nothing towards them without a good ground and warrant; but reafon not much with them: for I have over-much furfeited them with that, and *it is* not their fafhion to yeeld. And fuffer no conventions nor meetings among Church-men, but by your knowledge and permiffion.

Next the Scriptures, ftudie well your owne lawes: for how can yee difcerne by the thing yee know not? But preaffe to drawe all your lawes and proceffes, to be as fhort and plain as ye can: affure your felfe the long-fomneffe both of rights and proceffes, breedeth their un-fure loofeneffe and obfcuritie: the fhorteft being ever both the fureft and plainneft forme: and the long-fomneffe ferving onely for the enriching of the Advocates and Clerks, with the fpoyle of the whole countrie. And therefore delight to haunt your Seffion, and fpie carefullie their proceedings; taking good heed, if any briberie may bee tried among them; which cannot overfeverely be punifhed. Spare not to goe there, for gracing that farre any that ye favour, by your prefence to procure them expedition of Juftice: although that fhould

Of the lawes municipall.

Plat.4.de Rep.& 6. de Leg. Ar.1.rh.

Cic.1.de Or. Sen.in Lud.

Refort to the Seffion.

F 2   be

be speciallie done, for the poore that cannot waite on, or are debarred by migh-
tier parties.   But when ye are there, re-

Pla.in pol.
Arift.1.rh.
Cic.ad Q.
frat.
Plut.in If.
member the throne is Gods and not yours,
that ye fit in, and let no favour, nor whatfoever refpects move you from the right.
Ye fit not there, as I fhewed before, for
rewarding of friends or fervants; nor for
croffing of contemners, but onely for doing of juftice.   Learne alfo wifely to difcerne, betwixt juftice and equitie; and
for pitie of the poore, rob not the rich,
becaufe hee may better fpare it; but give
the little man the larger coat if it be his:
efchewing the errour of young *Cyrus* there-

Xen.1.Cyr. in.   For juftice, by the law, giveth every
man his owne; and equitie in things arbi-
trall, giveth everie one that which is meeteft for him.

But fpecial-
ly to the fe-
cret coun-
fell.
Be an ordinarie fitter in your fecret
counfell: that judicature is onely ordained for matters of eftate, and repreffing of
infolent oppreffions.   Make that judgement as compendious and plaine as yee
can; and fuffer no Advocates to bee heard

Cic.ad Q.
frat.
Tac.1.hif.
Plut.in De-
met.
there with their dilatours, but let everie
partie tell his owne tale himfelfe: and
wearie not to heare the complaints of the
oppreffed, *aut ne Rex fis*.   Remit everie
thing to the ordinary judicature, for efchewing of confufion: but let it bee your owne
craft, to take a fharpe account of every
man in his office.   And

And next the lawes, I would have you *Reading of* to be well verfed in authenticke hiftories, *hiftories.* and in the Chronicles of all Nations; but fpeciallie in our owne hiftories (*Ne fis pe-regrinus domi*) the example whereof moft neerely concernes you. I meane not of fuch infamous invectives, as *Buchanan's* or *Knoxe's* Chronicles: and if any of thefe infamous Libels remaine untill your daies, ufe the Law upon the keepers thereof. For in that poynt I would have you a Pytha-gorift, to thinke that the verie fpirites of *Plat.in* thefe archibelloufes of rebellion, have *Menon.* made tranfition in them that hoards their bookes, or maintaines their opinions; pu-nifhing them, even as it were their Au-thours rifen againe. But by reading of *Ar.1.rh.* authenticke hiftories and Chronicles, yee *Pol.1.* fhall learne experience by Theoricke, ap- *Plut.in* plying the by-paft things to the prefent *Timo.* eftate, *quia nihil novum fub fole:* fuch is *Ecclef.1.* the continuall volubilitie of things earthlie, according to the roundneffe of the world, and revolution of the heavenlie circles: which is expreffed by the wheeles in *Eze-* *Ezech.1.* *chiels* vifions, and counterfaited by the Poets *in rota Fortunæ.* And likewife by the knowledge of hiftories, ye fhall know how to behave your felfe to all Embaffa-dours and ftraungers; being able to dif-courfe with them upon the eftate of their owne countrie. And among all prophane

F 3   hifto-

hiftories, I muft not omit moft fpeciallie to recommend unto you, the Commentaries of *Cæfar*, both for the fweete flowing of the ftile, as alfo for the worthineffe of the matter it felfe. For I have ever bin of that opinion, that of all the Ethnicke Emperours, or great Captaines that ever was, he hath fartheft excelled, both in his practife, and in his præcepts in martiall affaires.

Of th'arts liberall. Sen.ep.84. As for the ftudie of other liberall artes and fciences, I would have you reafonablie verfed in them, but not preaffing to bee a paffe-maifter in any of them: for that cannot but diftract you from the points of your calling, as I fhewed you before: and when, by the enemie winning the towne, yee fhall bee interrupted in your demonftration, as *Archimedes* *Liu.l.24. Plut.in Marc.* was; your people (I thinke) will looke very bluntly upon it. I graunt it is meete ye have fome entrance, fpeciallie in the *Of Mathematickes. Pl.7.de leg. Ar.2. Metaph.* Mathematikes; for the knowledge of the arte militarie, in fituation of Campes, ordering of battels, making Fortifications, placing of batteries, or fuch like. And let not this your knowledge bee dead with*Jam.2.17.* out fruites, as S. *James* fpeaketh of Faith: but let it appeare in your daylie converfation, and in all the actions of your life.

Embrace

Embrace true Magnanimitie, not in being vindictive, which the corrupted judgements of the worlde thinkes to bee true Magnanimitie; but by the contrary, in thinking your offender not worthie of your wrath, empyring over your owne paſſion, and triumphing in the command-ing your ſelfe to forgive : husbanding the effectes of your courage and wrath, to be rightly employed upon repelling of inju-ries within, by revenge taking upon the oppreſſours, and in revenging injuries without, by juſt warres upon forraine ene-mies.   And ſo, where ye finde a notable injury, ſpare not to give courſe to the tor-rents of your wrath. *The wrath of a King, is like to the roring of a Lyon.*

Of magna-nimitie.
Ariſt.4. ath.
Sen.de cl.

Cic.1.Off.

Virg.6. Æn.

Pro.20.

Foſter true Humility , in banniſhing pride, not onely towardes God (conſider-ing yee differ not in ſtuffe, but in uſe, and that onely by his ordinance, from the ba-ſeſt of your people) but alſo towards your Parents.   And if it fall out that my Wife ſhall out-live me, as ever ye thinke to purchaſe my bleſſing, honour your Mother : ſet *Bathſheba* in a throne on your right hand : offend her for nothing, much leſſe wrong her : remember her

Of humi-litie.

Pl.4.de leg Xen.2.de dict.& fact.Soc.

> *Quæ longa decem tulerit faſtidia men-ſes;*

and that your fleſh and blood is made of hers: and beginne not, like the young

Lords

Lords and Lairds, your firſt warres upon your Mother; but preaſſe earneſtly to de-ſerve her bleſſing. Neither deceive your ſelfe with many that ſay, they care not for their Parents curſe, ſo they deſerve it not. O invert not the order of nature, by judging your ſuperiours, chiefly in your owne particular! But aſſure your ſelfe, the bleſſing or curſe of the Parents, hath almoſt ever a Prophetick power joyn-ed with it: and if there were no more, honour your Parents, for the lengthen-ing of your owne dayes, as God in his *Exod.20.* law promiſeth. Honour alſo them that *Xen.1.&* are *in loco Parentum* unto you, ſuch as *3.Cyr.* your governours, up-bringers, and Præ-ceptours: be thankfull unto them and reward them, which is your dutie and honour.

But on the other part, let not this true humilitie ſtay your high indignation to *Cic.ad Q.* appeare, when any great oppreſſours ſhall *frat.* præſume to come in your preſence; then frowne as ye ought. And in-caſe they uſe a colour of lawe in oppreſſing their poore ones, as over-many doe; that which *Ar.5.pol.* ye cannot mend by law, mend by the with-drawing of your countenance from them; and once in the yeare croſſe them, when their erands come in your way, re-compencing the oppreſſour, according to *Mat.18.* Chriſts parable of the two debtours.

Keepe

Keepe true Conſtancie, not onely in your kindeneſſe towards honeſt men; but being alſo *invicti animi* againſt all adver-ſities: not with that Stoicke inſenſible ſtu-piditie, where-with many in our dayes, preaſſing to winne honour, in imitating that auncient ſect, by their inconſtant be-haviour in their owne lives, belyes their profeſſion. But although ye are not a ſtocke, not to feele calamities; yet let not the feeling of them, ſo over-rule and doazen your reaſon, as may ſtay you from taking and uſing the beſt reſolution for remedie, that can be found out.

Of Conſtan-cie.
*Ar.*4.*eth.*
*Thuc.*3.6.
*Cic.*1.*Of.& ad Q.frat.*
Brut.ad Cic.

Uſe true liberalitie in rewarding the good, and beſtowing frankly for your ho-nour and weale: but with that propor-tionall diſcretion, that everie man may bee ſerved according to his meaſure: where-in reſpect muſt bee had to his ranke, de-ſerts, and neceſſitie. And provide how to have, but caſt not away without cauſe. In ſpeciall empaire not by your Liberali-tie the ordinarie rents of your crowne; whereby the eſtate royall of you, and your ſucceſſours, muſt bee maintained, *ne exhaurias fontem liberalitatis:* for that would ever be kept *ſacroſactum & extra commercium:* other-waies, your Liberali-tie would decline to Prodigalitie, in helping others with your and your ſucceſſors hurt. And above all, enrich not your ſelfe with

Of Libera-litie.
*Cic.*1.& 2.
Of.
Sal.in Jug.
*Sen.*4.*de ben.*

exactions

Isoc.ep.7.
Xen.8.Cyr.
Phil.Com.
10.

exactions upon your subjects; but thinke the riches of your people your best treasure, by the sinnes of offenders, where no prævention can availe, making justlie your commoditie. And in-case necessitie of warres, or other extraordinaries compell

Ar.5.pol.

you to lift Subsidies, do it as rarelie as yee can: employing it onely to the use it was ordained for; and using your selfe in that case, as *fidus depositarius* to your people.

And principallie, exercise true Wisedome; in discerning wisely betwixt true

Anent re-
porters.
Isi. ad Ph.
in Panath.
& de per.
Cic.ad Q.fr.
Plut.de cu-
rios.

and false reports: first, considering the nature of the person reporter: next, what entresse he can have in the weale or evill of him, of whom hee maketh the report: thirdlie, the likelie-hoode of the purpose it selfe; and last, the nature and by-past life of the dilated person: and where yee finde a tratler, away with him. And although it be true, that a Prince can never without secrecie do great things, yet it is better oft-times to try reportes, then by credulity to foster suspition upon a honest man.

Isde pac.
Cic.3.Of.

For since suspition is the Tyrants sicknesse, as the fruites of an evill Conscience, *potius in alteram partem peccato*: I meane, in not mistrusting one, whom-to no such unhonestie was knowne before. But as for such as have slipped before, former experience may justly breede prævention by fore-sight.

And

And to conclude my advice anent your behaviour in your perſon; conſider that God is the author of all vertue, having imprinted in mens mindes by the very *Cic.3.Tuſc* light of nature, the love of all morall vertues; as was ſeene by the vertuous lives of the olde Romaines: and preaſſe then to ſhine as farre before your people, in all vertue and honeſtie; as in greatneſſe of ranke : that the uſe thereof in all your actions, may turne, with time, to a naturall habitude in you; and as by their hearing of your lawes, ſo by their ſight of your perſon, both their eyes and their eares, may leade and allure them to the love of vertue, and hatred of vice.

ΒΑΣΙ-

ΒΑΣΙΛΙΚΟΝ ΔΩΡΟΝ.

OF A

KING's

BEHAVIOUR

IN

INDIFFERENT THINGS.

Book the third.

IT is a true old saying, That a King is *C.ph.8.3.* as one set on a stage, whose smallest *de leg.* actions and gestures, all the people *Ovid. ad* gazinglie doe behold : and therefore al- *Liu.* though a King be never so precise in the *Quint.4.* discharging of his office, the people, who *decl.* seeth but the outward part, will ever judge of the substance, by the circumstances ; and according to the outward appearance, if his behaviour bee light or dissolute, will conceive preoccupied conceits of the Kings inward intention : which although with time, the triar of all trueth,

it

it will evanish, by the evidence of the contrarie effectes, yet *Interim patitur justus*; and prejudged conceits will, in the meane time breede contempt, the mother of rebellion and disorder. And besides

Indifferent actions and their dependancie.
Plato in Phil.& 9. de leg.

that, it is certaine that all the indifferent actions and behaviour of a man, have a certaine holding and dependance, either upon vertue or vice, according as they are used or ruled: for there is not a middes betwixt them, no more then betwixt their rewards, heaven and hell.

Be carefull then, my Sonne, so to frame al your indifferent actions and outward behaviour, as they may serve for the furtherance and foorth-setting of your inward vertuous disposition.

Two sorts of them.

The whole indifferent actions of a man, I devide in two sorts: in his behaviour in things necessary, as foode, sleeping, rayment, speaking, writing, and gesture; and in things not necessarie, though convenient and lawfull, as pastimes or exercises, and using of companie for recreation.

First sort and how they be indifferent

As to the indifferent things necessarie, although that of themselves they cannot be wanted, and so in that case are not indifferent; as likewaies in case they be not used with moderation, declining so to the extremitie which is vice; yet the qualitie and forme of using them, may smell of

vertue

vertue or vice, and be great furtherers. to any of them.

To beginne then at the things neceſſarie; one of the publickeſt indifferent actions of a King, and that manieſt, eſpeciallie ſtrangers, will narrowlie take heede to; is his manner of refection at his Table, *Formes at the Table.* and his behaviour thereat.   Therefore, as Kings uſe oft to eate publikelie, it is meete *Xen. in Cyr.* and honourable that ye alſo doe ſo, as well to eſchew the opinion that yee love not to haunt companie, which is one of the markes of a Tyrant; as likewiſe, that your delight to eate privatelie, bee not thought to bee for private ſatisfying of your gluttonie; which ye would bee aſhamed ſhould be publikelie ſeene.   Let your Table bee honourablie ſerved ; but ſerve your appetite with fewe diſhes, as young *Cyrus* did: which both is holeſom- *Xen. 1. Cyr* meſt, and freeſt from the vice of delicacie, which is a degree of gluttonie.   And uſe *Plut. in A-* moſt to eate of reaſonable groſſe , and *pophth.* common-meates; aſwell for making your body ſtrong and durable for travell at all occaſions, either in peace or in warre; as that yee may be the hartlier received by your meane ſubjects in their houſes, when their cheere may ſuffice you: which other-waies would be imputed to you for pride and daintineſſe, and breede coldneſſe and diſdaine in them.   Let all your foode be

simple,

Sen.ep.96.
simple, without compofition or fauces; which are more like medecines then meate. The ufing of them was counted amongft the auncient Romanes a filthie vice of de-licacie; becaufe they ferve only for plea-Sen. de con-fol.ad Alb. Juven. fat. 2. fing of the tafte, and not for fatisfying of the neceffitie of nature: abhorring *Api-cius* their owne citizen, for his vice of .de-Arift.4. eth. licacie and monftrous gluttonie. Like as both the Græcians and Romanes had in deteftation the verie name of *Philoxenus*, for his filthy wifh of a Crane-craig. And therefore was that fentence ufed amongft Xen.de dict. & fact. Socr. Laert. in Socr. Cic.5.Tuf. Plat.6.de Leg. Plin.l.14. them againft thefe artificiall falfe appetites, *optimum condimentum fames.* But bee warre with ufing exceffe of meat and drinke; and chieflie, beware of drunken-neffe, which is a beaftlie vice, namelie in a King: but fpeciallie bewarre with it, be-caufe it is one of thofe vices that increafeth with age. In the forme of your meat-eat-ing, be neither uncivill, like a groffe Cy-nick; nor affectately mignard, like a dain-tie dame; but eate in a manlie, round, Cic.1.Of. and honeft fafhion. It is no waies comely to difpatch affaires, or to be penfive at meate: but keep then an open and cheere-ful countenance, caufing to reade pleafant hiftories unto you, that profite may bee mixed with pleafure: and when yee are not difpofed, entertaine pleafant, quicke, but honeft difcourfes.

And

And becaufe meate provoketh fleeping, *Of fleepe,* be alfo moderate in your fleepe; for it go- *Pla.7.de* eth much by ufe: and remember that if *leg.* your whole life were divided in foure parts, three of them would bee found to be confumed on meate, drink, fleepe, and unneceffarie occupations.

But albeit ordinarie times would com- monlie bee kept in meate and fleepe; yet ufe your felfe fome-times fo, that any *Beft forme* time in the four and twentie houres may *of diet.* bee alike to you for any of them; that thereby your diet may be accommodate to your affaires, and not your affaires to your diet: not therefore ufing your felfe to over great foftneffe and delicacie in your fleepe, more then in your meate; and fpeciallie in-cafe yee have adoe with the warres.

Let not your Chalmer bee throng and *Formes in* common in the time of your reft, afwell *the Chal-* for comelineffe, as for efchewing of car- *mer.* rying reports out of the fame. Let them that have the credite to ferve in your Chalmer, bee truftie and fecrete; for a King will have neede to ufe fecrecie in ma- ny things: but yet behave your felfe fo in your greateft fecrets, as ye neede not bee afhamed, fuppofe they were all proclaim- ed at the mercate croffe. But fpecially fee that thofe of your Chalmer bee of a founde fame, and without blemifh.

G   Take

Dreames not to be taken heed
Take no heede to any of your dreames: for all Prophecies, visions, and prophetick dreames are accomplished and ceased in Christ. And therefore take no heede to freets either in dreames, or any other things: for that errour proceedeth of ignorance, and is unworthy of a christian; who should bee assured, *Omnia esse pura puris*, as *Paule* saieth; all daies and meates being alike to Christians.

Rom. 14. Tit. 1.

Of apparell.
Next followeth to speake of rayment, the on putting whereof is the ordinary action that followeth next to sleepe. Be

Iſo. de reg.
also moderate in your rayment; neither over superfluous, like a deboshed waister; nor yet over base, like a miserable wretch; not artificiallie trimmed and decked, like a Courtizane; nor yet over sluggishly cloathed, like a countrie-clowne; not over lightly, like a Candy-fouldier, or a vaine young Courtier; nor yet over gravelie, like

Cic. 1. Of.
a Minister. But in your garments be proper, cleanlie, comely and honest: wearing your cloathes in a carelesse, yet comelie forme: keeping in them a middle forme, *inter Togatos & Paludatos*; betwixt the gravitie of the one, and lightnesse of the other. Thereby to signifie, that by your calling ye are mixed of both the professi-

Plu. de reg.
ons; *Togatus*, as a Judge making and pronouncing the lawe; *Paludatus*, by the power of the sword: as your office is like-

wise

wife mixed, betwixt the Ecclefiaticall and Civill eftate. For a King is not *merè lai-cus*, as both the Papiftes and Anabaptiftes would have him ; to the which error alfo the Puritanes incline overfarre. But to returne to the purpofe of garments, they ought to bee ufed according to their firft inftitution by God; which was for three caufes: firft, to hide our nakedneffe and fhame: next and confequentlie, to make us more comelie: and thirdly, to preferve us from the injuries of heate and colde. If to hide our nakednes and fhameful parts, then thefe naturall parts ordained to be hid, fhould not be reprefented by any undecent formes in the cloathes: and if they fhould help our comelines, they fhould not then by their painted preened fafhion, ferve for baites to filthie lecherie; as falfe haire and fairding does amongft unchafte wo-men : and if they fhould preferve us from the injuries of heate and colde, men fhould not, like fenfeleffe-ftones, contemne God, in light-lying the feafons; glorying to con-quer honour on heate and cold. And al-though it be praife-worthie and neceffarie in a Prince, to be *patiens algoris & æftus*, when he fhall have adoe with warres upon the fields : yet I thinke it meeter that ye goe both cloathed and armed, then naked to the battell; except you would make you light for away-running: and yet for cowards, *metus addit alas.* And ſhortlie in your cloathes keepe a proportion, as well with the ſeaſons of the yeare, as of your age: in the faſhions of them being careleſſe, uſing them according to the *Cic.1.Of.* common forme of the time, ſome-times richlier, ſome-times meanlier cloathed as occaſion ſerveth, without keeping any *Ar. ad Alex.* preciſe rule therein. For if your minde be found occupied upon them, it will be thought idle otherwaies, and yee ſhall be accompted in the number of one of theſe *compti juvenes*; which will make your ſpirit and judgement to be leſſe thought of. But ſpeciallie eſchew to bee effœminate in your cloathes, in perfuming, preening, or ſuch like: and faile never in time of warres to be galliardeſt and braveſt, both in cloathes and countenance. And make not a foole of your ſelfe in diſguiſing or wearing long haire or nailes; which are but excrements of nature, and bewray ſuch miſuſers of them, to be either of a vindictive, or a vaine light naturall. Eſpecially, make no vowes in ſuch vaine and outward things, as concerne either meate or cloathes.

What ordinarie armour to be uſed at Court. Let your ſelfe and all your Court weare no ordinarie armour with your cloathes, but ſuch as is Knightlie, and honourable: I meane Rapier-ſwords, and daggers. For tuilyeſome weapons in the Court, betokens con-

confufion in the countrey. And therefore banifhe not onely from your Court,
all trayterous offenfive weapons, forbid-
den by the lawes; as Gunnes and fuch
like (whereof I fpake alreadie) but alfo
all trayterous defenfive Armes, as Secrets,
Plate-fleeves, and fuch like unfeene armour. For, befides that the wearers
thereof, may be præfuppofed to have a
fecrete evill intention, they want both the
ufes that defenfive armour is ordained for:
which is, to bee able to holde out vio-
lence, and by their outwarde glaunfing in
their enemies eies, to ftrike a terrour in
their harts. Where by the contrarie, they
can ferve for neither ; being not onely un-
able to refift, but dangerous for fhots, and
giving no outwarde fhow againft the enemie : being onely ordained, for betraying
under truft; whereof honeft men fhould
be afhamed to beare the outwarde badge,
not refembling the thing they are not.
And for anfwere againft thefe arguments,
I know none but the old Scottes fafhion :
which if it be wrong, is no more to
bee allowed for auncientneffe, then the
old Maffe is, which alfo our forefathers
ufed.

The next thing that yee have to take *Of language*
heede to, is your fpeaking and language; *and gefture.*
whereunto I joyne your gefture, fince *Ar.3.ad Theod.*
action is one of the cheefeft qualities, that *Cic.in o₁ ad Q.fr & ad B*

is required in an oratour : for as the tongue
speaketh to the eares, so doth the gesture
speake to the eyes of the auditour.   In
both your speaking and your gesture, use
Cic.1.Of. a naturall and plaine forme, not fairded
with artifice: for (as the French-men say)
Rien contre-faict fin : but eschewe all affec-
tate formes in both.

In your language be plaine, honest, na-
Id. eod. turall, comely, cleane, short, and senten-
cious : eschew both the extremities, aswell
in not using any rusticall corrupt leide, as
booke-language, and penne and inke-horne
tearmes : and least of al mignarde and effœminate tearmes.   But let the greatest part
of your eloquence consist in a naturall,
Id.ad Q. cleare, and sensible forme of the deliverie
frat. & of your minde, builded ever upon cer-
ad Brut. taine and good groundes ; tempering it
with gravitie, quicknes, or merines, according to the subject, and occasion of the
time ; not taunting in Theologie, nor
alleadging and prophaning the Scripture
in drinking purposes, as over manie doe.

Id.1.Of. Use also the like forme in your gesture ;
neither looking sillely, like a stupide pe-
dant ; nor unsetledly, with an uncouth
morgue, like a new-com-over Cavalier: but
let your behaviour be naturall, grave, and
according to the fashion of the countrie.
Phil.ad A- Be not over-sparing in your courtesies ;
lex.
Cic.2.Of. for that will be imputed to in-civility and
arro-

arrogancie: nor yet over prodigall in jow-
king or nodding at every ſtep; for that
forme of being populare, becommeth bet-
ter aſpiring *Abſalons*, then lawfull Kings: *Ariſt.4.*
framing ever your geſture according to *Æth.*
your preſent actions: looking gravelie *Cic.ad At.*
and with a majeſtie when yet ſit in judgement, or give audience to Embaſſadours;
homely, when ye are in private with your
owne ſervantes; merelie, when ye are at
any paſtime or merrie diſcourſe; and let
your countenance ſmell of courage and
magnanimitie when yee are at the warres.
And remember (I ſay over againe) to bee *If.de reg.&*
plaine and ſenſible in your language: for *in Evag.*
beſides that it is the tongues office, to be
the meſſenger of the mind; it may bee
thought a point of imbecilitie of ſpirite
in a King, to ſpeake obſcurelie; much *Cic.3 Of.*
more untrulie: as if hee ſtoode awe of any
in uttering his thoughts.

Remember alſo, to put a difference betwixt your forme of language in reaſon- *Id.1.Of.*
ing, and your pronouncing of ſentences,
or declaratour of your will in judgement, *Formes in*
or anie otherwaies in the points of your *reaſoning.*
office. For in the former caſe, ye muſt
reaſon pleaſantlie and patientlie, not like a
King, but like a private man and a ſcho-
·ler: otherwaies, your impacience of contradiction will be interpreted to be for
lacke of reaſon on your part. Where in

the

the points of your office, ye should ripe-lie advise indeede, before ye give forth your sentence: but fra it be given forth, the suffering of any contradiction, dimi-nisheth the Majestie of your authoritie, and maketh the processes endlesse. The like forme would also be observed by all your inferiour judges and Magistrates.

In judge-ment.
Is. ad Nic.
Cic. ad Q.
frat.

Now as to your writing, which is no-thing else, but a forme of en-registrate speech; use a plaine, short, but statelie stile, both in your Proclamations and mis-sives, especiallie to forraine Princes. And if your engine spurre you to write any workes, either in verse or in prose; I can-not but allow you to practise it : but take no longsome workes in hande, for distra-cting you from your calling.

Of writing,
and what
stile fitteth
Princes.

Flatter not your selfe in your labours, but before they be set foorth, let them first bee privilie censured by some of the best skilled men in that craft, that in these workes ye meddle with. And because your writes will remaine as true pictures of your minde, to all posterities; let them be free of all uncomelinesse and unhonestie: and according to *Horace* his counsell,

Cic. 1. Of.

Nonumque premantur in annum.
I meane both your verse and your prose; letting first that fury and heate, where-with they were written, coole at leasure; and then as an uncouth judge and censor,

De arte
Poetica.

revising

reviſing them over againe, before they be publiſhed, *quia neſcit vox miſſa reverti.* *Id. eod.*

If yee would write worthilie, chooſe ſubjectes worthie of you, that be not full of vanitie, but of vertue; eſchewing obſcuritie, and delighting ever to bee plaine and ſenſible. And if ye write in verſe, remember that it is not the principall part of a poëme to rime right, and flow well with many pretie wordes: but the chiefe commendation of a poëme is, that when the verſe ſhall be ſhaken ſundrie in proſe, it *Ar.de art.* ſhall be found ſo rich in quicke inventions, *poet.* and poëticke flowers, and in faire and pertinent compariſons; as it ſhall retaine the luſtre of a poëme, although in proſe. And I would alſo adviſe you to write in your owne language: for there is nothing left to be ſaid in Greeke and Latine alreadie; and ynewe of poore ſchollers would match you in theſe languages: and beſides that it beſt becommeth a King to purifie and make famous his owne tongue, wherein he may goe before all his ſubjects; as it ſetteth him well to doe in all honeſt and lawfull things.

And amongſt all unneceſſarie things that are lawfull and expedient, I thinke exerciſes of the bodie moſt commendable *Of the ex-* to bee uſed by a young Prince, in ſuch ho- *erciſe of the* *bodie.* neſt games or paſtimes, as may further *Xen.1.Cyr.* abilitie and maintaine health. For albeit I

graunt

graunt it to bee moſt requiſite for a King to exerciſe his engine, which ſurely with idleneſſe will ruſt and become blunt; yet certainlie bodily exerciſes and games are verie commendable, as well for baniſhing of idleneſſe (the mother of all vice) as for making his bodie able and durable for travell, which is verie neceſſarie for a King. But from this count I debarre al rough and violent exerciſes, as the foot-ball; mæeter for laming, then making able the uſers thereof: as likewiſe ſuch tumbling trickes as onely ſerve for Comedians and Balladines, to winne their bread with. But the exerciſes that I would have you to uſe (although but moderatelie, not making a craft of them) are running, leaping, wraſtling, fencing, dauncing, and playing at the caitch or tenniſe, archerie, palle maillé, and ſuch like other faire and pleaſant field games. And the honourableſt and moſt commendable games that yee can uſe, are on horſeback: for it becommeth a Prince beſt of anie man, to be a faire and good horſeman. Uſe therefore to ride and danton great and couragious horſes; that I may ſay of you, as *Philip* ſaid of great *Alexander* his ſonne, Μακεδονία ȣ σε χωρεῖ. And ſpecially uſe ſuch games on horſeback, as may teach you to handle your armes thereon; ſuch as the Tilt, the Ring, and low-riding for handling of your ſword.

Plat.6.de leg.
Ar.7.&8. pol.
Cic.1.Of.

Pl. eod.

Xen.in Cyr.
Iſ.de jug.

Plut.in Alex.

I

I cannot omit heere the hunting, name- *Of hunting.*
ly with running hounds; which is the
moſt honourable and nobleſt ſort thereof:
for it is a theeviſh forme of hunting to
ſhoote with gunnes and bowes; and
Greyhound hunting is not ſo martiall a
game. But becauſe I would not be thought
a partiall praiſer of this ſport, I remit you
to *Xenophon*, an old and famous writer, *In Cyn. 1.*
who had no minde of flattering you or *Cyr. & de*
me in this purpoſe: and who alſo ſetteth *Rep. Lac.*
downe a faire paterne, for the education *Cic. 1. Of.*
of a young King, under the ſuppoſed *Cyropædia.*
name of *Cyrus*.

As for Hawking I condemne it not, but *Of Haw-*
I muſt praiſe it more ſparinglie; becauſe *king.*
it neither reſembleth the warres ſo neere
as hunting doth, in making a man hardie,
and skilfullie ridden in all grounds; and
is more uncertaine and ſubject to miſ-
chances: and (which is worſt of all) is
there-through an extreame ſtirrer up of
paſſions. But in uſing either of theſe
games obſerve that moderation, that ye
ſlip not there-with the houres appointed
for your affaires, which yee ought ever *Ar. 10.*
preciſelie to keepe: remembring that *Æth.*
theſe games are but ordained for you, in
enabling you for your office, for the which
yee are ordained.

And as for ſitting houſe paſtimes, where- *Of houſe*
with men by driving time, ſpur a free and *games.*

faſt

faſt enough running horſe, (as the proverbe is) although they are not profitable for the exerciſe either of minde or bodie, yet can I not utterlie condemne them; ſince they may at times ſupplie the roome, which being emptie, would be patent to pernitious idleneſſe, *quia nihil poteſt eſſe vacuum.* I will not therefore agree with the curioſitie of ſome learned men in our age, in forbidding Cards, Dice, and other ſuch like games of hazard: although otherwaies ſurely I reverence them as notable and godlie men. For they are deceived therein, in founding their argument upon a miſtaken ground; which is, that the playing at ſuch games, is a kinde of caſting of lot, and therefore unlawfull; wherein they deceive themſelves. For the caſting of lot was uſed for triall of the trueth in any obſcure thing, that otherwaies could not bee gotten cleered; and therefore was a ſort of prophecie: where by the contrarie, no man goeth to theſe playes, to cleere anie obſcure trueth, but onelie to gage ſo much of his owne money, as he pleaſeth, upon the hazard of the running of the cardes or dice, as well as hee would doe upon the ſpeede of a horſe or a dogge, or any ſuch like gaigeour. And ſo, if they bee unlawfull, all gaigeours upon uncertainties muſt likewaies be condemned. Not that thereby I take the

defence

Ar.8.pol.

Dan.de luſ. al.

rumpunt bonos mores colloquia prava. And chiefly abſtaine from haunting before your *Men.* mariage, the idle companie of dames, which are nothing elſe, but *irritamenta libidinis.* Beware likewiſe to abuſe your ſelfe in making your ſporters your coun- ſellers: and delight not to keepe ordina- rilie in your company, Comœdians or Balladines: for the Tyrants delighted moſt *Pl.3.de rep* *Ar.7.&* in them, glorying to be both authors and *8.pol.* actors of Comœdies and Tragœdies them- *Sen.1.ep.* ſelves. Where-upon the anſwere that the *Dyoniſ.* Poet *Philoxenus* diſdainefully gave to the Tyrant of *Syracuſe* there-anent, is now come in a proverbe, *reduc me in latomias.* *Suid.* And all the ruſe that *Nero* made of him- ſelfe when he died, was *Qualis artifex pe-* *Suet.in* *reo?* meaning of his skill in menſtraſlie, *Ner.* and playing of Tragœdies: as indeed his whole life and death, was all but one Tragrœdie.

Delight not alſo to bee in your owne perſon a player upon inſtruments; eſpe- cially on ſuch as commonly men winne their living with: nor yet to be fine of any mechanicke craft: *Leur eſprit s'en* *1.Sept.* *fuit au bout des doigts,* ſaith *Du Bartas:* whoſe workes, as they are all moſt wor- thie to be reade by any Prince, or other good Chriſtian; ſo would I eſpeciallie wiſh you to be well verſed in them. But ſpare not ſometimes by merrie companie,

to be free from importunitie: for yee
should be ever mooved with reason, which
is the onely qualitie whereby men differ
from beasts; and not with importunitie.

Curt.8.

For the which cause (as also for augment-
ing your Majestie) yee shall not bee so
facile of accesse-giving at all times, as I

Liu.35.
Xen.in
Ages.
Cic.ad Q.
frat.

have beene: and yet not altogether reti-
red or locked up, like the Kings of *Persia*:
appointing also certaine houres for publike
audience.

A speciall
good rule in
govern-
ment.

And since my trust is, that GOD hath
ordained you for moe Kingdomes then this
(as I have oft alreadie sayd) preasse by the
outward behaviour as well of your owne
person, as of your Court, in all indifferent things, to allure peece and peece, the
rest of your Kingdomes, to follow the fa-
shions of that Kingdome of yours, that
ye finde most civill, easiest to be ruled,
and most obedient to the lawes. For these
outward and indifferent things, will serve
greatly for allurements to the people, to
embrace and follow vertue.   But beware
of thrawing or constraining them thereto; letting it be brought on with time,
and at leasure: specially by so mixing
through alliance and daily conversation,
the inhabitants of every Kingdome with
other, as may with time make them to
growe and weld all in one.   Which may
easilie be done betwixt these two nations,
                                    being

Lightning Source UK Ltd.
Milton Keynes UK
UKOW06f0324050814

236350UK00010BA/752/P